The Next Revolution

Francis Browne

CONTENTS

Introduction

I guess it's a question we've all asked ourselves at some time or another,"*What is it that is driving the changes to our world?*" Surprisingly, a lot and the thing is, it's those seemingly small changes that have crept up on us that have the potential of profoundly changing the world we live in. Changes that we just accept and then ignore. If we stay oblivious to these small changes, we become ignorant in the decisions we make, decisions that can affect whole generations to come. Take for example, the 2016 Brexit referendum in the UK. Although it seemed to be a small and insignificant event in the scheme of things, it actually has a major impact on the future of people's lives across the globe. The same can be said of the 2017 election of Donald Trump to the White House in America. So, we have to ask ourselves, why is this change happening? Why has change accelerated in recent times? And why, given the growing discontent in the world, have we allowed these changes to continue unabated?

Throughout history, we've seen major changes that have had real impact on the lives of ordinary citizens. Back in the 14th century we had the French Revolution. This was probably the most famous of all bloody revolts by ordinary citizens against an authoritarian regime. Of course, there have been other notable revolutions since then, such as the Bolshevik uprising against the Tzar of

Russia in 1917. That revolution saw the demise of Russian Royalty and directly led to the formation of an equally brutal communist regime in the form of the USSR in 1922. This was a revolution that had a great impact on the modern world as a whole. It also brought the British Monarchy into conflict with the then British Prime Minister David Lloyd George. The British Government of the time had agreed to grant asylum to the Romanov family in the UK. However, King George V and his consort, Queen Mary, vehemently opposed the idea, even though the two Royal households were directly related.

In 1989, the world witnessed the Romanian Revolution, another citizen-led revolt that culminated in the overthrow of a communist regime and the execution of Nicolae and Elena Ceaușescu. In more recent times, revolutions have been a little more peaceful. One that I personally witnessed was the Ukrainian Orange revolution of 2004/2005. This revolution was more of a series of public demonstrations and civil resistance rather than the violent revolutions of the past. However, it did culminate in a change of government in Ukraine with very little bloodshed. Unfortunately, the same could not be said of the second Ukrainian revolution of 2014 which was called the Euromaidan revolution. This revolt was marred by a series of violent clashes between protestors and riot police. But, the resulting ousting of Viktor Yanukovych once again demonstrated that popular revolt can still get results.

The problem with the Euromaidan revolution is that it directly led to the annexation of Crimea, civil unrest and conflict in the East of Ukraine, and brought Russia back into direct conflict with the West. Clearly, not a good outcome.

If we look at modern history, there have been a number of events that have had a direct impact on the way we live today. World War II, 9/11, The advent of the European Union, the rise of extremism in the Arab world and globalisation. All these things have had a direct impact on the way we think and the way in which we decide what is good for us and what is a potential disaster waiting to happen. Whilst all these seemingly unimportant events maybe considered historic in terms of their individual impact on the world we live in today, over time and with a cumulative effect, we are beginning to realise that we are no longer in control of our destinies. Instead, we take all these events in our stride by either embracing them, or being totally abhorred by them, but we do very little to protest about the effects they may have on our longer term well being. When we look back at World War II, we know that was a terrible chapter of our history that led to the deaths of many people from many countries. When it was all over, we all had a vision of a better future. One that wouldn't involve us in armed conflict ever again. The reality is that it just hasn't happened. However, our demands for change to the way in which we conduct ourselves within an international community has directly led us into new areas of conflict. Maybe not the sort of conflict that leads to mass bloodshed, but certainly conflict that has the potential of leading to a new form of citizen revolt.

The thorny subject of the European Union and its apparent undemocratic rule over much of continental Europe was a direct descendent of our desire to avoid future world wars, particularly in Europe. It was born from the ashes of World War II and is still having an impact on the lives of European citizens today. The EU experiment is now reaching a point where ordinary citizens are starting to revolt against its wide reaching, bureaucratic structures and its escalating administrative costs. What started out as a seemingly well intentioned concept has now become a major and divisive debate among European citizens, one that is likely to spill over into a far more serious Europe-wide revolt in the not too distant future.

The events of 9/11 in the USA were probably the biggest wake-up call we ever had. It shook the world to its core. We had a sudden realisation that not everyone in the world actually liked our so-called democratic bubble. Over 3,000 people died in a single day as a direct result of one single act of terrorism. This was yet another event that triggered shouts for change from the citizens of the free world, but did we really get the sort of change we demanded? No, we ended up invading Iraq who had absolutely nothing to do with the atrocities of

9/11. That act of aggression towards Iraq in itself caused a mild revolution as the world suddenly woke up to the fact that the invasion of Iraq, a country that had all the military might of a rolled-up newspaper, was actually little more than a Bush-Blair agenda for regime change in a country that had been a thorn in the side of Western democracies for years. 9/11 and the demands of citizens to do something about it was the catalyst that the US and UK administrations needed to fulfil their personal agenda and launch an all-out invasion of a sovereign state. Yet, despite all the public calls for action over 9/11, very few people actually demanded to know why the US was so violently attacked in the first place. What was it that caused an extremist group to murder thousands of people in a single act of gross terrorism? If we could find the answer to this one question, we may be better placed to solve the problems of extremist violence that we all face today.

The financial crash of 2008 was yet another event that sparked a mild revolution from the public. Not since the Great Depression of the 1930's had ordinary people seen the economic rape of whole economies and individuals. Suddenly, we started to understand that major financial institutions around the world had been given carte blanch by our democratically elected governments to steal money on a grand scale. Again, the revolutionaries of the world demanded change, and change we got. Instead of throwing all the crooks in jail, our politicians singled out a handful of lowly-paid employees for criminal prosecution and then used our money to bail out the real crooks so they could do it all over again. It's not the change we wanted, but it is change which is set to fuel more public dissatisfaction in the future. Financial deprivation in the world has always been a big contributor to revolutions. In our modern world, all the danger signals are starting to emerge again, only this time on a scale that is unprecedented. The success of national economies are no longer judged by their real wealth, they're judged by their ability to build massive debts that can only be serviced by continually increased spending by consumers. In 2017, the national debt of the USA was standing at over $20 trillion. The UK's debt surpassed £1 trillion, and Germany, a country considered to be one of the wealthiest in Europe, had a national debt of €2.2 trillion. The Eurozone as a whole has a whopping debt burden of almost €10 trillion. These are eye-watering figures. Despite this huge piling-up of debt in the world's major economies, we hear of privately owned global corporations amassing billions in annual profits whilst the less well-to-do of the world are sliding deeper and deeper into abject poverty.

Other factors have also seen their way into the mix. Added to all of the above concerns we have globalisation. A strange phenomenon that is on target to really tip the balance in favour of a future revolution. We now live in a world where a relatively small handful of major corporations, particularly high-tech companies, have seemingly been granted more powers than the world's security services to collect data on the lives of each and every one of us. They use the information to sell us stuff that we simply don't need. It's a system designed to force us into spending vast amounts of money to bolster the mismanaged economies of the world. What is really strange is that these mega corporations all seem to have been established by fresh-faced students straight out of college. The whole globalisation system is making billionaires out of young people in their early to mid twenties and giving them massive powers over the lives of ordinary people. They operate huge data-centres that would put the security services of major world powers to shame. They collect, hold, sell and distribute information about each and every one of us. They target us with a constant stream of advertising messages designed specifically to encourage us into believing that all is right with the world as long as we keep buying "stuff". Of course, as ordinary citizens who simply view all this snooping and mind conditioning as a form of progress that we should embrace, we are highly critical of those countries where their populations are shielded from this onslaught of mass exploitation. We in the West call it censorship and oppression, but is it really?

Although many people haven't realised it yet, these mega corporations are actually controlling many facets of our lives, but what is really strange is that many of us voluntarily sign-up for this mass intrusion into our private lives. Our insatiable appetite for new technologies has resulted in the absolute surrender of our privacy, something that no government could ever achieve through legislation. Once the "penny drops" and people start to understand what is really happening to them, there will be a different type of "digital" revolution. One in which ordinary citizens will simply abandon the established technology and seek alternative methods of communication, like speaking to each other.

Globalisation has also seen a massive shift of wealth from the purses of ordinary citizens into the hands of a few very wealthy people on the planet. Even in Communist China, where all people are supposed to be equal, we see a high concentration of some of the world's wealthiest people. They are using their great wealth to acquire vast quantities of business and property assets across the world. Whilst governments are quite happy to absorb this vast spending to help keep economies afloat, the ordinary citizens are increasingly finding themselves priced out of markets dealing with the essentials of life, such as housing and basic food. For governments who continue to ignore this escalating invasion on the well-being of their own citizens, revolution will surely come, giving those governments some seriously heavy problems to deal with.

We are now where we are. At the time of writing this book it was 2017. We've observed everything that has happened to us since the end of World War II and we are starting to get "twitchy". A revolution is coming and many of us know it. There is only so much that the great unwashed of the world can accept as a "fait accompli" The world is starting to wake up again and is ready to confront those that wish to exercise total control over the masses. It will, inevitably, lead to revolution. Not necessarily the bloody revolutions we've seen in the past where politicians Royalty and dictators get dragged into the streets for public execution, but certainly a revolution that will change the course of history yet again. Hopefully, through the pages of this book, I can explain in simple terms what is really happening in today's world. We will be examining all the facets of our lives discussed above to better understand how they are so intertwined that the whole system will have to be completely dismantled if we are to stand any chance of creating a happy world for future generations. Armed with this information, you will be better placed to make your voice heard (*preferably at the ballot boxes of the world rather than in the streets*). Knowing what it is that has lead us to a world of discontent allows us to focus on issues that are important in changing our current direction. Just like generations before us, we cannot afford to stand still and simply accept everything that our political masters throw at us. We should learn to question, to look beyond the immediate action being proposed and start analysing what the end game really is. By having a basic understanding of our changing world and the agenda that our political leaders have in store for us, we will be better placed to make our voices heard in a civilised and democratic manner. It may be a quiet revolution, but a revolution it will be. It's starting to happen as this book is being written. The bloody revolts of the past won't be necessary. Social media will ensure that effective action can be taken to guarantee the rights of our children and their children. All we need to do is understand what's going on around us today and make decisions based on our own instincts. It's all too easy in today's world to just sit back and be dictated to by a bunch of career politicians. Start thinking for yourself, form an opinion and act accordingly. When it comes to future change, it can be change for the better, but only if you are part of that inevitable next revolution.

In the next chapter of this book, I'm going to go to some length to give any younger readers the benefit of some historical insights into the world we live in today. It isn't the historical facts as such that are important, but more about the way in which the modern world has had its thinking manipulated by politicians. Modern history has led many of us to believe just about everything we are told by those who are often perceived as being more wise than the rest of us. This trust in our politicians has been so enshrined into our education and upbringing that in today's world we've become over reliant on our political masters in telling us the truth about everything that happens in our modern everyday lives. By examining modern history we can gain a better insight into how manipulating facts to better suit political agendas creates a more controllable public opinion. We've all been conditioned to accept everything that we are told as being gospel. So, treat the next chapter as a history of current human conditioning. Understand how our historic past has been used to condition us into believing everything we're told and you will have a better understanding of how the modern world, both political and commercial, is exploiting us today.

In the Beginning

We're going to start our analysis of the changing world we live in today with World War II. This is the one event in our modern history that really set the ground for many of the situations we find ourselves in today. World War II established allies and enemies that would stay locked together for many, many years. It was also an event that was triggered by circumstances not too dissimilar to those we are facing today. Although Hitler's rise to power spanned many years between the world wars, it was against a backdrop of perceived social injustice, the rise of nationalism, world economic problems, feelings of anti-capitalism and the promotion of anti-semitism that Hitler was able to seize power. He used traditional methods of persuasion, such as legitimate political campaigning, along with some atrocious violent street battles. But, power he got, and once he had Germany under his control he set about his domination of Europe as a whole. His initial secret pact with Soviet leader Joseph Stalin would have probably enabled Hitler to realise his dream of global domination. As it happened, the two of them had a serious falling out over Poland which led to the USSR changing sides and joining the allies in bringing about the downfall of Hitler.

This one historic event is largely responsible for the animosity between today's Russia and the West. When we look back at World War II, it can be safely said that the USSR suffered the greatest loss of life in bringing the war to an end. Some twenty million Russians died in the conflict, almost twice as many as all the other European countries involved put together. It could also be argued that Russia was instrumental in causing the surrender of Japan to the USA in 1945. This controversial piece of history centres around the fact that then US president Harry Truman struck a deal with Joseph Stalin that would see a full scale land invasion of Japanese held territories by the USSR. With hindsight, the US president changed his mind, but somehow forgot to enlighten his Soviet counterpart to the change of plan. Instead, Truman was persuaded to test a new atomic weapon, the likes of which the world had never seen before. Of course, it was a double whammy for Truman because not only could he get to test the "A" bomb on a ruthless regime in Japan, but he could also send a message to Stalin and the USSR that America wasn't to be messed with. And so it was, on August 6th 1945, the Americans detonated their atomic bomb over the city of Hiroshima. It was two days later on August 8th that the Soviets decided to formally declare war on Japan. The following day the USSR invaded the Japanese State of Manchukuo. That same day, America dropped its second bomb on Nagasaki. Although history records that it was the dropping of these two bombs that caused the Japanese to surrender on August 15th, other schools of thought have emerged that suggest it wasn't the devastation and loss of human life caused by the atomic bombs that prompted the surrender of Japan at all. After all, the controlling powers of Japan were not particularly well known for their humanity, particularly when it came to their own people. Historians are now suggesting that it was the potential loss of Japanese culture, sovereignty, and the potential dismantling of the Japanese dynasty that caused the surrender to the allies. This school of thought holds some credence when you consider it was six days after the Nagasaki bombing when the surrender finally came. The choice was to either surrender to an invading USSR or surrender to the USA. Clearly, had Japan surrendered to the USSR, Japan would have completely lost its national identity and culture which would have seen it replaced with a communist dictatorship that would have been difficult for the Japanese to stomach. So the decision was made to surrender to the USA who would, at least, guarantee the maintenance of all things dear to the Japanese.

Now that the war in Europe and the Pacific was technically over, there next came the division of spoils between the USSR and the other allies. For its part, the USSR started its invasion of Korea on the day it declared war on Japan. At that time Korea was Japanese territory, so the invasion was perfectly in line with the promises the USSR made to join the allies in the Pacific War at the Yalta conference in February 1945. However, the USA was worried that the USSR would advance rapidly and engulf the whole of Korea which, as Japanese territory, had been surrendered to the allies. So, on August the 10th the US government suggested a demarkation line to be known as the 38th parallel. This line would act as a natural division between a USSR controlled North Korea and an Allied controlled South Korea. It's a division that still exists today and is classed as the most heavily militarised zone in the world. Much to everyone's surprise, the USSR accepted the proposed division and went about their business of occupying the northern territories.

Meanwhile, over in Europe, another share of the spoils operation was underway. This was a little more complicated because the USSR had already decided that many eastern European states would fall under the influence of Moscow by effectively turning them into communist satellite States. These States were, in effect, acting as a buffer zone to prevent the possibility of another German attack and to block the USSR from open contact with the West. This came to be known as The Iron Curtain. Germany itself was carved up into 4 zones and although it was only to be a temporary arrangement, it resulted in the ultimate creation of two German states, the Federal Republic of Germany (West Germany) and the German Democratic Republic (East Germany). West Germany was actually the amalgamation of 3 zones, each controlled by one of the allied powers at the time, namely the British, the French and the Americans. In response, the Soviets created East Germany out of the zone they were awarded at the end of the war. The rest, as they say, is history.

The culmination of this tragic period of modern history was actually the beginning of many issues that we face today. Although the Soviets were our allies during the war, they became the bad boys when the fighting was over. This was largely due to disagreements over the way Europe had been carved up and the European fear of an increasing sphere of influence it gave to the USSR. This ultimately led to the Cold War which has been going on in one form or another right up until today. The animosity between today's Russia and the West hasn't been helped by other conflicts that have sprung up between the end of World War II and today. The US led covert operations in Afghanistan against the USSR which started in 1979 may have been one of the biggest mistakes ever made by the West. Not only was the USA financing militant Islamic groups in order to prolong the war with the USSR, it also led to the ultimate defeat of the USSR. One has to ask the question if the USSR had been allowed to continue without covert interference from America, would we be facing the terrorist threats of today?   It's no wonder that the Russians wouldn't support the US in its invasion of Iraq and Afghanistan after 9/11.

Today's Russia is also somewhat bitter towards the West for a number of other reasons. The West has never really acknowledged the importance of USSR involvement in bringing the Second World War to an end, nor the massive loss of Russian life suffered as a result of the conflict. In fact, the whole world has generally been led to believe that it was the USA stepping in at the 11th hour that tipped the balance in favour of the allies. Whilst we cannot overlook the importance of America's role in bringing the war to an end, they don't really deserve the accolade of being the "driving force" of the German surrender. In fact, when we examine the American led conflicts that have occurred since the end of World War II, not one of them has resulted in a good outcome, let alone any that could be remotely considered a victory. So, whilst the West pats itself on the back on every anniversary of "Peace in Europe," everyone conveniently forgets the role of the former USSR. Now I'm not suggesting for one moment that Stalin was a nice guy who had the interests of the rest of the world at heart, but he was a man who commanded a military force that gave great assistance to the West with the objectives of freeing Europe from the clutches of a madman, and restoring a degree of calm in the Pacific. So, the least we could do is to acknowledge the role of USSR and its people in a more positive light. Sadly, that has never really happened and so we face a continuing cold war to this day.

All that should have changed in December 1991 when then Soviet president Mikhail Gorbachev dissolved the

Soviet Union, an act that acknowledged independence of the Soviet Republics. This created the Commonwealth of Independent States and included Armenia, Georgia, Lithuania, Turkmenistan, Azerbaijan, Kazakhstan, Moldova, Ukraine, Belarus, Kyrgyzstan, Russia, Uzbekistan, Estonia, Latvia and Tajikistan. This single act helped foster a new relationship with the West. Then US president Ronald Reagan, although viewed by some at the time as being a bit of a "flakey" president, actually proved to be instrumental in cementing a much more subdued relationship with Russia. As for the Russian people, they were, initially, quite happy to go along with the new cordial relationship with the West. After all, up until that point, many Russians had a degree of envy towards the West. It should also be noted that Russians in general never had any real animosity towards the West at all. The animosity was very much something of the West's making which was caused by fear in Europe and the US that the Soviet Union would cause a shift in political attitudes towards a more communist ideology. Ordinary Russians, however, had no such fear of the West. We had all the trappings of choice. We could elect our own governments, buy the food, clothing and homes that we wanted, we were free to make our own way in life by establishing our own businesses and generally enjoyed all the trappings that successful economies could bestow on their respective populations. Russians, on the other hand, were forced to endure a life of having the State provide everything from the cradle to the grave and in return they would have to give up their lives to the service of the State. For its part, the Russian government never actually propagated the notion that the West was a threat to Russia except in terms that their precious Iron Curtain was essential to the prevention of future hostilities. After all, it was Germany that spilled over into the borders of Russia and caused so much human carnage. So, the Russians had every reason to fear the West as a potential invading force. Unfortunately, to counter the potential rise of communism as a political choice in the West, the US and Europe generally, fed us the notion that Russia was dangerous and could attack us, not only militarily, but also through our way of life should communism become a serious contender in our political structures. They are still feeding us that line today.

Meanwhile, in the new Russia that emerged under Gorbachev, ordinary Russians were given the opportunity to experience and participate in a democracy for the first time in their lives. The capitalist world came knocking at Russia's door and almost everyone embraced the new found opportunities presented by this dramatic social change. Inevitably, there were more losers than winners as this change emerged. A small handful of Russians became seriously wealthy whilst the vast majority of the population suddenly realised they no longer had the protection of the State in providing for their basic needs. They were now forced to make their own way in life, to be responsible for their own ability to earn money and create opportunities that could enhance their lifestyle. This was a massive change that led many ordinary Russians to believe that capitalism wasn't all it was cracked-up to be. That was the point at which resentment of the West started to creep into the Russian psyche. There was a sudden realisation that life wasn't going to be a walk in the park under a capitalist regime.

Although many younger Russians enjoyed the trappings of their new found freedoms and embraced the ability to have choice in their lives, such as the ability to buy modern fashion brands, new luxury vehicles, a wide choice of international foods and the relative freedom to travel the world, many of the older generation of Russians were becoming insecure. They could no longer rely on the State for basic essentials, they were being left behind in this new capitalist world they had been thrust into. This led Russians to become more sceptical of western ideals. It was against this backdrop that the world saw the rise of President Vladimir Putin. His popularity among Russians (*about 85%*) was largely due to the growing resentment of the West by ordinary Russians who were experiencing the typically western phenomenon of the "rich getting richer and the poor getting poorer".

Speaking about her Nobel Prize-winning book in 2015, Svetlana Alexievich observed why Vladimir Putin had gained such popularity among Russians generally. She was quoted as saying that a lot can change in Russia over five years, but nothing changes over 200 years. This adequately explains why Putin won overwhelming public support when he was re-elected to office in 2012. During his first term as president and subsequent term as prime minister, Putin presided over a Russia that witnessed phenomenal economic growth for a straight eight years. However, when he stood for a second term in 2012 he understood that the mood of the people had changed. So, instead of promising the electorate greater economic growth, better living standards, higher employment, greater levels of social care and all the other facets of modern Russian life that was causing so much resentment among the older generation, he changed tactics completely. He promised to create a strong Russia that would be respected in the world, a Russia that could stand up for itself and wouldn't be dictated to by the West, a Russia that would restore Russian culture and social values and resist the politically correct ideals of the West. In other words, he promised the population a slice of the past. Of course, recent history has shown that he was good to his word (*unusual in the world of politics!*). His forays into Ukraine, Georgia, Syria and the annexation of Crimea were designed specifically to send a message to the West that Russia was back with a vengeance. These acts of aggression made Putin even more popular with ordinary Russians, especially in view of the fact that Putin now controlled the Russian media which enabled him to put any spin he liked on these events and the Russian public would simply buy it for no other reason than there was little or no opposing media coverage within the country.

This change of tactic did, of course, come at a price for Russia. The economy tanked, due in part to economic sanctions being imposed on Russia by the West. Despite those sanctions being aimed squarely at the political elite and big business, Putin arbitrarily decided to impose tit-for-tat sanctions on the West by limiting or banning the importation of foodstuffs from the USA and Europe. Sadly, these sanctions only served to punish ordinary Russian citizens as they suddenly couldn't find certain foreign foods in the stores. This, in turn, led to local producers capitalising on the situation by charging higher prices for locally produced equivalents. The end result has been soaring inflation and a reduction in living standards.

The reason I've gone to some length to explain the situation in Russia is that it is indicative of the new type of politics that's creeping through the world at the moment. If I step back for a moment to 1982, you may recall that Britain, under the premiership of Margaret Thatcher, sent the British fleet to retake the Falkland Islands after an invasion of the territory by Argentina.

This was direct retaliation for a real act of aggression by Argentina. As such, Margaret Thatcher won the wholehearted support of the British people and the respect of many other countries around the world. What today's Russia highlights is that there is no longer any need for a real act of aggression to spark popular support for a political leader. Instead, politicians can simply imply aggression so that the people stand behind them in full support of everything they do. What is more troubling is that they do it to win domestic support so they can retain power and control over their own country. Ukraine, Georgia, and Syria have never invaded Russia or acted aggressively towards Russia (*not militarily anyway*) and yet we see the Russian people standing firmly behind their political masters in full support of every single act of aggression that Russia has been responsible for in recent years. Russia, of course, is not alone in this. Even in the United States under George W. Bush and the UK under the premiership of Tony Blair, we witnessed the invasion of a sovereign state on the basis of "Spin". Aka, the invasion of Iraq. However, unlike Russia, neither the USA or their allies the UK had control over the media, so it all went a bit pear-shaped when vast swathes of the US and UK populations opposed the war in highly significant numbers. So, although politicians may attempt to stoke up domestic support for their personal aims and ambitions by creating mythical acts of aggression that have to be dealt with militarily, it doesn't work in a society that has freedom of the press. But, we have to ask the question, how long will it be before western democracies DO take control of the media and deny us the opportunity of opposing anything they do? Hopefully, we're too far down the line for that to happen so we still have the opportunity to set our own revolutionary agenda. Russia, on the other hand, is not a full democracy yet. It's a very insular society that is more easily controlled by the powers that be. It has been referred to as a "tandemocracy" in which the President controls the prime minister and if their roles are reversed (*as happened in 2008 when Dmitry Medvedev became president and Putin became prime minister*), the outgoing president still calls the shots. This is a very dangerous situation for the world at large because there is little the international community can do to change the situation.

Another prime example of "aggression for domestic support" is North Korea. Although this is a pure dictatorship, it is still important for the people to stand behind their political leaders. If that were not the case, the international community could take aggressive action on the basis that they were freeing North Koreans from the tyranny of their dictatorial leader. Of course, if the North Korean people are in full support of their leader (*whether through indoctrination or free thought*), there would be very little point in the international community taking any action against

North Korea until such time as a mass admission by North Korean citizens that they are living under severe oppression occurs. Strangely, we in the West have, and still are, being indoctrinated into believing that North Korea is a serious threat to our well-being. The reality is that North Korea has never invaded or attacked another country in its entire history. The closest they came to becoming an invading force was when they attempted to take-back South Korea in 1950. That doesn't mean to say that it won't pose a serious international threat in the future. What it does show is that despite being a dictatorship, it still needs the popular support of its citizens as a precursor to rattling its sabre on the international stage. Likewise, Western democracies also have to use the fear factor in their domestic arenas in order to win support for potential retaliation. In 2017, we witnessed North Korea testing the range of it's missile systems as a direct provocation to the West. Whilst many people will agree that the North Korean leadership is "barking mad", very few people actually believe that they would launch a suicidal first-strike on another country. But, that didn't stop then US president Donald Trump from engaging in "fighting talk" with the North Korean dictatorship. What most western politicians have understood is that a war of words with a provocative nation is going to win them domestic support and enable them to maintain power. It also enables the "selling" of a potential threat to the domestic audience as a means of getting the public on-board if retaliation is ultimately needed.

In concluding our historic analysis of how we've arrived at the state of today's world I think we can summarise the situation very simply. We have the USA, who is still expected to sort out the world's problems. They, like most countries of the world, are leaning strongly towards "kidology" as a means of getting public support for potential future military actions. Then we have Russia that is in full control of public thinking and have taken the first brazen steps to instigate serious problems where none existed. Then we have Europe in the form of the European Union. This quarter of the world is a form of unelected Federal State who have won the military reputation of having a "bark worse than its bite". Then we have North Korea and it's perceived threat to the civilised world (*could be real or otherwise*). Finally, we have the middle East and Asia (*including Turkey*). This area of the world is fast becoming the playing field of conflicts where the big nations can play war games without them directly threatening the security of their own citizens. Its almost like the world has become a game of chess where all the nations of the world are the pieces and the Middle East /Asian regions represent the chess board on which the world will enact their wars against each other.

The reason that we find ourselves in this precarious situation is all about economic power. It's a strange anomaly that nations that suffer great economic downturns are more likely to use international conflicts as a means of maintaining domestic power at home. Countries that are perceived to be more economically affluent tend to maintain popularity momentum by selling us even more economic growth. This is what has happened in countries like Russia. During their time of economic growth there was little or no threat to the outside world. Unfortunately, because economic growth was restricted to the chosen few, it became an unpopular ticket upon which to maintain domestic power. Therefore, asserting power over other nations and using propaganda at home to stimulate continued political support was the way Russia could deflect attention away from its domestic affairs. This is the start of a slippery slope to international isolation. As international sanctions start to bite, the economy recedes, making it even more urgent to maintain an aggressive stance in the rest of the world. However, there does come a time in this downward cycle when the population wakes-up and rebel against their political leaders - normally after a prolonged period of suffering and well after the international damage has been inflicted.

In western democracies, a similar thing is taking place. We see vast wealth being created by a small section of society whilst the majority start feeling the pain of decreasing affluence. This too is a dangerous situation that could well lead to the same "Russian-like" sabre-rattling we've experienced in recent years. The need will be for politicians to deflect attention away from economics and to focus our attention onto nationalistic pride. Defence of the nation against fairy-tale threats will surpass common logic. If the politicians win us over, they will retain power, but the downside will be that they will have to make good on their promises. They will have to invoke acts of aggression in order to save face and prove to the domestic audience that they were right to alert us to the potential dangers posed by other countries. Hopefully, our currently free and open media will prevent us from being totally hoodwinked and allow us to see through the spin. It's only the determined will of ordinary people that can prevent "kidology" from taking us down a path we don't wish to travel. We do have the power to sack those politicians who would use us as pawns to pursue personal power objectives. If we can force ourselves to see through the "smoke and mirrors" of political shenanigans we will be better placed to start and finish the next revolution. If you think a revolution is unnecessary in a civilised, democratic society, think again. The only difference between a democracy and a dictatorship is that in a democracy you get to elect your dictator. If there was ever a prime example of this in action, just look at the aftermath of the UK Brexit referendum in 2016. In this landmark referendum the majority of the British electorate voted to withdraw from the European Union. They wanted to regain control of British borders and bring to a halt the wasteful bureaucracy of an unelected Federal European government. However, the remain camp in that referendum *(the minority)* just couldn't allow themselves to accept the democratic decision of the British electorate. Mainstream pro-European opposition parties vowed to disrupt the business of government if the decision wasn't reversed, or they weren't given the right to approve the terms under which the UK would leave the EU. Succumbing to such threats would inevitably result in a watered down Brexit that would still leave Britain's borders open and leave the country exposed to many of Europe's bureaucratic rules and regulations. As a consequence Britain's then prime minister, Theresa May, was forced into holding an early general election in order to secure a fresh mandate to take Britain out of the EU. In the run up to that election we saw all the pro-European opposition parties instilling the fear factor into the minds of the British electorate. They were hell-bent on ignoring the wishes of the majority in favour of appeasing the minority - they wanted to become elected dictators. And, all because they wanted political power on their terms and let the majority be damned. This is the way modern career politicians work in today's democracies. They invoke fear to get power so they can dictate to the majority. In political terminology, it's called "dividing the nation", a selfish act that puts egoistic megalomaniacs into powerful positions. As it happened, British Prime minister Theresa May saw her government's majority reduced after calling the general election. Such is the power of fear mongering. She didn't get the enhanced mandate she was hoping for in her negotiations on the terms of Britain's exit from the EU. Instead, she had to form a pact with a minority political party as a means of getting legislation through parliament and to keep the disruptive politicians at bay.

So, the first and most important phase of our next revolution will be to tackle these narrow-minded politicians and start seeing through their rhetoric. These are the people who will divide a nation to the point that ordinary citizens will be at each other's throats over issues that only serve the interests of the political elite. They are the sort of people who have, historically, driven countries to civil war. They are little more than selfish megalomaniacs who will do anything to secure their petty existence in a position of power. If we can resist the temptation of believing them simply because they have a nice demeanour, we will be well on our way to resolving many of the problems the world is facing today. It may be many years away, particularly in those more insular societies ruled by dictators and the like. But, just like Germany after World War II, the people will eventually see the light and realise they had been lied to all along. Let's just hope it doesn't take another major conflict to wake us all up.

The Great Economic Myth

Before we get too deeply entrenched in the world of economics, lets start by looking more closely at that word "economic". What does it mean? In its original literal sense it meant the careful management of resources. Nowadays, there are two words to contend with. The first word is "economical" which retains the meaning stated above. The other word is "economic" which, in the modern world, means something entirely different. It means the financial management of an economy, as in "the government's economic policy". Given that the word economical is a derivative of the word economic, we can only assume that the changing meaning of the latter is a deliberate attempt at confusing us into believing that economic is some kind of good thing that makes us all wealthier through the prudent management of money. The sad reality is that in today's world it means just the opposite. Technically speaking, the term "economic growth" should mean a growth in prudent money management when, in fact, its meaning is now considered to be the growth in money supply and reckless spending.

To put it simply, economic growth means more and more consumer spending. Essentially, we buy "stuff" we don't need with money that we don't have. Instead, we borrow money from banks who then expect us to spend our lives slavishly working to earn sufficient money in the future with which to repay the borrowing. In a nutshell, the more we can borrow against the promise of our future earnings, the more "stuff" we can buy. This keeps the manufacturers of all that "stuff" in business and allows them to employ more people, thus creating more spending power which can be used to purchase even more "stuff" that people don't need and to create even more tax revenues for governments. It's a vicious circle and is becoming a difficult economic model to sustain in today's world.

To fully understand what money is and how it works, let's start with a very simplistic scenario. Assume a village with a population of one thousand people. One day a dollar bill mysteriously arrives in the hands of one of the villagers. Now assume that a voice in the villager's head convinces him that this dollar bill can be used to buy something he needs instead of bartering goods and services. The first thing the villager decides he needs is a chicken for Sunday lunch, so he goes off to his neighbour and convinces the chicken farmer that this dollar is worth one chicken and the farmer can subsequently use the dollar bill to buy something that *he* needs. So the deal is struck and the original owner of the dollar bill goes home with his Sunday lunch. So, what just happened? Well, the one dollar bill has now been given a value - it's worth one chicken. So, the chicken farmer will be looking for something to buy with his one dollar bill that he would ordinarily acquire in exchange for a single chicken, so he goes to his neighbour, a dairy farmer, and persuades him to take the one dollar in exchange for a gallon of milk. The dairy farmer, in turn, exchanges the one dollar for a bag of wheat from his neighbour. This process continues until the entire village has taken possession of the dollar bill and its found its way back to the original owner who starts the whole process over again.

What this illustrates is that this single dollar in circulation has created one thousand dollars of spending power purely based on the value attributed to it by the first owner. This is called money circulation and illustrates perfectly how a small amount of cash can create quite substantial spending power through circulation. It also illustrates that money has no real value other than the value attributed to it through its use as a medium of exchange in which a real-world asset is purchased.

Let's now go a step further with this scenario. Assume that the one dollar bill arrived in the hands of a would-be banker who had absolutely no need to exchange it for any product or commodity. Being a banker, he spots an opportunity to exploit the situation, so he decides to lend the dollar to the chicken farmer at 10% interest. The chicken farmer now starts the money-go round by purchasing his gallon of milk from the dairy farmer. He, in turn goes off to buy his bag of wheat and so the cycle continues until the dollar bill is back in the hands of the chicken farmer. Now that he has the dollar back in his possession, he decides to repay the banker, but there's a problem. Because there is only a single dollar bill in circulation, there is no way the farmer can repay the 10% interest on the money - it simply doesn't exist, even though that single dollar has created one thousand dollars worth of buying power. The banker's only option is to foreclose on the chicken farmer and take one of his chickens in settlement of the debt. The problem is that the banker can't sell the chicken to get his 10% interest because there is no more money in circulation. So, the whole lending for interest thing comes to a sticky end. Sound familiar? It should do because this is exactly what happened in the financial crash of 2007/2008, only on a much grander scale. You see, if there is no new money being created as money circulates, it becomes impossible for banks to collect interest on money they've lent.

One of the problems in the modern world is quite simply that ordinary people, or very few of them, actually understand money and what it is. To many people, money has a tangible value based on a real commodity (*it used to be gold*). Whilst this was generally the case when money originally became the preferred means of exchange, it isn't the case in today's world. All the notes and coinage in the world today are simple tokens that represent buying power - they have no real value other than the paper or metal they are made from. The other general misconception is that when you deposit your token money in a bank, it somehow finds its way into a huge piggy-bank in the back office where it is retained until you go and withdraw it. During the interim period, it is often assumed that the banks can dip into this piggy-bank of token deposits to make loans to other people. Of course, both of these notions are completely wrong. What actually happens is that when you deposit money into a bank account, it becomes the bank's money. In return the bank gives you an IOU in the form of a bank account upon which they enter the value of your deposit, basically converting your cash deposit into a number on a computer screen which you can spend through your debit card or by drawing cash tokens from an ATM.

When it comes to bank loans, the bank doesn't actually touch their depositor's money at all. Instead, they create new money that gets put into circulation. This is possible by virtue of the bank's balance-sheet. In the case of a deposit, your cash is entered onto the Asset side of the bank's balance-sheet (*remember, it's now their money*) and in order to balance the books the bank also enters the amount of the deposit on the Liabilities side of the balance-sheet (*the liability being your bank account acknowledging the bank's liability to repay your deposit*). This ensures that the balance-sheet is in balance i.e. assets minus liabilities should equal zero (*ask any accountant*). When it comes to loans, exactly the same thing happens. In order to obtain a loan you will have to enter into a loan agreement with the bank. That agreement will involve a pledge of real world assets with which to secure the loan. The agreement itself now becomes an asset of the bank and is entered on the Asset side of the balance-sheet. The actual loan amount is then added to your account and appears on the liabilities side of the balance sheet. Again, assets minus liabilities should equal zero. So, at the stroke of a pen, the bank can create new money in the form of a loan as long as they have a corresponding asset to add to their balance-sheet (*your secured loan agreement*). If you still doubt the accuracy of this explanation, just think about this. Less than 3% of all the money in the world today is in the form of notes or coin. If banks only had this 3% available from which to make loans, they would quickly run out of money and all lending would come to a grinding halt until such time as outstanding loans had been repaid in full. Furthermore, if all the depositors who paid that 3% into the world's banks went back to withdraw their money, there would be none left because it would have all been loaned out.

For the purpose of clarity, it should be noted that although we talk about a single bank in the above example, we are in fact, talking about the banking system as a whole. Every day millions of transactions in the form of credits and debits are undertaken which, if left unchecked, would upset the balance-sheets of individual banks. To correct the problem a central bank steps into the picture to restore the balance-sheets of its banks. It does this by automatically debiting and crediting the reserve accounts of individual banks. Reserve accounts are essentially notional accounts that simply display the value of all of a bank's assets (*not just physical cash*). By totalling all the money owed to a particular bank at the end of a day's transactions, and deducting all the amounts owed by that bank to other banks, the Central bank arrives at figures which can be debited or credited to all the accounts involved. This simply involves moving numbers from one computerised account to another. In the event that one or more banks is left with a shortfall on its balance-sheet (*liabilities exceed assets*), those banks can borrow money from the banks that have a surplus (*assets exceed liabilities*). This is called interbank borrowing. As can be seen, the whole banking system is essentially one big bank, therefore it's relatively easy to keep all the banks solvent and in good shape. That is until something goes drastically wrong.

Back in 2007/2008 the world witnessed the virtual collapse of the financial system, largely due to the greed of big banks. What happened is that the banks realised they could make a fortune by lending (*creating*) money against overvalued real world assets and make those loans available to people who couldn't adequately service the loan repayments. It all started in the USA, but had a swift knock-on effect around the world - and here's why.

Banks started granting home loans for amounts greater than the real value of the properties being purchased. They also lent recklessly to people with low credit ratings. To be sure that they wouldn't be left holding the baby when the loans were defaulted, the banks packaged all their dodgy loans into financial instruments that could be sold on to the investment markets. In order to attract serious money for these instruments, the banks cut a deal with the rating agencies under which the banks would pay a fee to have a "triple A" rating attached to their instruments. This allowed pension funds, investment companies and even local and national governments around the world to buy these instruments as long-term investments. The sale of these instruments made a lot of people very wealthy indeed. Investment banks in particular did extremely well by packaging and marketing these junk instruments to the world's investors. The original lending banks also made a nice tidy profit from the scam. So, where did it all go wrong?

Technically speaking, the whole scam would have probably gone unnoticed had it not been for a downturn in the economy. Generally, what happened was that the repayments on all those dodgy loans couldn't be met which forced the mortgage holders to foreclose on the properties. This, in turn, created a massive problem as thousands of people found themselves homeless, some even became jobless. This rendered those people un-creditworthy, they could no longer borrow money. If they couldn't borrow, the banks couldn't create new money through the creation of loans. When money supply slows down in this way, the knock-on effect is devastating. A huge reduction in spending power results in people buying less "stuff" that they don't need. This results in manufacturers, wholesalers and retailers cutting back production and supply of consumer products which, in turn, leads to unemployment. This reduces spending power even further and renders a whole new group of people un-creditworthy. The problem was compounded by the fact that all those foreclosed properties were worth less than their declared balance sheet value. What's more, the value was further declining at a rapid pace because there were more homes for sale than the economy could utilise (*mainly due to the inability of banks to create new loans*). In other words, supply exceeded demand which resulted in further reductions in values.

In balance-sheet terms, the investment banks suddenly saw a massive fall in the value of the real world assets they were holding. Furthermore, no loan repayments were coming in with which to top up the balance-sheet. At the same time, their liabilities to investors was increasing. So, the point was reached where the liabilities exceeded the asset value on the balance-sheets of the major investment banking institutions, essentially making them insolvent. They suddenly found themselves in the position of our villager banker who was stuck with a chicken and no opportunity to sell it to someone else - the money simply wasn't there.

The longer term outcome of this self inflicted financial crisis was just as devastating as the front-line effects of the crisis itself. In order to overcome the problem, the governments of the world decided to bail-out many of the affected companies and financial institutions. The answer was to simply create new money in the form of government securities (*IOU's*) which could be lodged with the central banks so they could rebalance the books of these failed institutions. The problem is, government notes have to be repaid at some time - they are simply IOU's. The only way that most governments can meet the liabilities of these notes is to collect more taxes from ordinary working people. This is because a government's only source of income is taxation of one sort or another. In some countries, notably the UK, the government took ownership of the institutions they bailed-out with the intention that when they returned to profitability they could sell the government's stake in the open markets, hopefully for a profit. But, for the most part, many people will end up paying the price of this failed financial system for generations to come.

Although the financial system appears to have been restored, There is a strong probability it will happen again in the future, only on a much larger scale. By bailing-out the crooks, governments have literally given the financial markets carte blanche to do it all over again. But because governments will most likely need to collect more taxes to cover the liability of the bail-out notes, they need to see an exponential rise in economic growth. Without such growth, there will simply not be enough money sloshing around the system to be taxed. The problem with exponential growth is that it's unsustainable - something has to give if another financial crash is to be avoided in the future. To illustrate the madness of the current thinking I'm going to borrow an example from Dr. Albert Bartlett of the University of Colorado. He used the analogy of bacteria dividing in a laboratory jar. The first bacterium divides and becomes two. They divide and become four and so it continues. Now assume it's 11:00 am when the first bacterium is placed in the jar and that they double in number every minute. At 12:00 midday, the jar is full. The question the good Dr. then posed was "At what time was the jar half full?" The answer of course is 11.59. Because with just one minute to go, the half full jar of bacterium will double and fill the jar completely. The second question posed was "If you were an average bacterium in that jar, at what time would you realise you were running out of space?" Clearly, if you were sitting in that jar at 11.59 you wouldn't necessarily see a problem. You may think it's taken 59 minutes to reach this point and we still have half the space still available - you may not even think about it. Certainly, if you'd taken a look round after 56 minutes you definitely wouldn't see a problem coming because the jar would only be 6.3% full. But lets assume one of the bacterium in the jar started alerting all the others to a pending space problem. All the other bacterium would probably laugh and say "What are you talking about - we have all this space left, there is no problem". But the fact is in just four minutes the jar will be full and at crisis point. Now lets assume that at a few seconds before midday, the alarm eventually goes off. Space is rapidly running out and a state of emergency is declared. In steps the government with a bail-out plan. They pull a new jar out of the hat and all the bacterium breathe a sigh of relief as they start flowing into the new jar. But guess what? At 12:01 the new jar is suddenly full, so the government steps in again with two new jars. Again, one minute later at 12:02 all four jars are full. So, although it took a full 59 minutes to realise that space was becoming a problem and despite the drastic and valiant bail-out efforts of the bacterium government, it took only a total of three minutes for the problem to return at quadruple the original size. The alarming aspect of this analogy is that the problem will continue to increase in size every minute thereafter and will require a string of bail-out plans, each twice as large as the previous one.

Now lets go back to economics. Instead of talking about bacterium, lets start talking about economic growth. Lets convert those minutes into years. Most of the world will sit by and think "it's taken 59 years to half fill our economic jar so we have nothing to worry about in terms of economic growth". The first simplistic reaction will be to assume it's going to take another 59 years before we have a problem, remember, the economic jar is only half full. However, just one year later an economic bail-out is needed in order to sustain current levels of growth. 2 years later, another bail out of twice the size of the previous one is needed and a further two jars are found to maintain the level of growth in the economy. What this illustrates is the very real danger of exponential growth. In economic terms growth is all about spending power. The ability to continue buying consumer goods in greater quantities. However, in order to buy these goods, someone has to make them and everything that is manufactured on planet earth starts life as a natural resource. So, in order to sustain economic exponential growth we have to use up ever increasing quantities of natural resources. It may be good for employment figures because all this manufacturing activity creates jobs. Extra jobs equates to greater money supply through the payment of salaries. Our politicians assume that's good for the economy because they can collect even more payroll taxes, VAT or sales tax on all that extra money. All they now have to do is maintain that growth momentum. In the modern world this happens by making consumer goods obsolete before they've reached the end of their useful life. Already we see this with new technology products being released a year or two after the release of a preceding product. Look at smartphones as a prime example. After one or two years you throw away a perfectly good smartphone so you can buy the latest model. We see it in other areas of the modern world. We are encouraged through clever marketing and sometimes through government incentives to replace automobiles far more frequently than we have to. Domestic appliances often break down after 2 years. We should be asking ourselves is this by accident or by design? We are constantly being encouraged to buy more food than we consume - just look around any modern supermarket at all the special price jumbo packs and two for one offers. Clearly, something has to break and my fear is that it will happen sooner rather than later. Every time we are forced into economic crisis management mode, we will inevitably see a return of the problem more frequently and at higher levels.

Now, you're probably wondering what all this has to do with the next revolution. Well, put simply, it will all be down to distribution of wealth and the rape of natural resources around the world. Certain countries of the world cannot sustain themselves with only the natural resources they have. Therefore, there will be incursions into other territories to get those all important resources. This could well lead to major conflicts erupting as the world's larger and more powerful nations seek to exploit resources in other countries that may not be too disposed to letting them go. We've seen it with oil and gas. As the big powerful nations consume more and more energy, they start looking to other countries to fuel their appetite for these limited resources. If they can't get those resources on good commercial terms, they will attempt to take them by force.

Manufacturing industries are becoming massive global empires that can keep the world flooded with an ever increasing variety of consumer goods and services. Much of this manufacturing power is concentrated in places like Asia where the sourcing of manufactured goods is relatively cheap. However, these global companies are more likely to concentrate their sales and marketing efforts in the wealthier economies of the world where they can sell these cheaply sourced goods at vastly inflated prices. Governments, as you would expect, actively encourage this situation because it keeps that money-go-round continually flowing and expanding. They then congratulate themselves on boosting the economic growth and prosperity of their respective nations. The reality is they are just stock-pilling a massive problem for future generations to solve. It should also be remembered that the more we continue to manufacture, the more natural resources have to be harvested to keep the production lines going. At the same time, we are creating huge mountains of redundant products that are not easy to recycle in any meaningful way. A similar situation is happening in the world of agriculture. People more eminent than I have already observed that we appear to be able to grow and harvest enough food to feed the estimated 70 billion farm animals of the world (*which are largely used to feed the more affluent countries of the planet*) and yet we are unable to grow and harvest sufficient food to feed the 7.5 billion or so human population of the world. It's utter madness and, if left unchecked, it will only be a matter of time before ordinary people begin to see the light and revolt against this seemingly pointless attempt at spending our way to non-existence. That spending is also what is enslaving the world. Because we are constantly making "stuff" that we don't need, we have to borrow money to buy it all. That borrowing is essentially allowing us to spend our future earnings today, enslaving us to a life of work just to keep the financial system alive and kicking.

So, now we have a better understanding of how economics work, we should maybe take a look at how we've allowed our economies to become so driven by mythical money management and the often times madness of economic growth. How have we become so misled into believing that that the fallacy of economic growth is somehow the "great good" that many of us view it to be? The answer, of course, lies in the "WIIFM" factor - What's In It For Me. Every great corporation started life as a dream - a vision in the minds of their originators. Companies like Microsoft, Apple, Google, Amazon, Starbucks, Kentucky Fried Chicken and McDonalds, all started life as concepts dreamed up by their respective founders. But, in order to make these companies into the successful household names they've become today required money. That money came from investors who shared the dream. People who were sold on the vision of success and wealth creation that these companies conjured up and a promise to share the profits with their investors. The promise of "money for nothing" has almost universal appeal and investment is one way to achieve wealth without actually doing any work. It's this WIIFM factor that encourages ordinary people to gamble, whether it be at the casino, or in the financial markets. This is not a bad thing in itself but, it is the reality of the commercial world we live in today. We are actively encouraged to use our surplus money to invest in visionary enterprises that can create jobs, create wealth and fulfil social needs whilst at the same time fulfilling our WIIFM needs. Of course, if we don't have any surplus money, the banks will normally lend it to us. Many governments will even offer tax breaks to encourage us to keep investing into new enterprises that have the potential of becoming the next major industries that will help keep the money supply bubble inflating at an ever increasing rate. The problem is that few people, particularly politicians, ever expected these companies to become so dominant that they could threaten the world order of money supply and creation. This has created a great conundrum for governments the world over. Many of these companies have profits that exceed the tax revenues of many countries around the world. The fortunes of people like Microsoft's Bill

Gates could have solved the Greek National Debt crisis (*as of 2015*) out of small change. (*this doesn't account for the total of Greek debt at the time - it only accounts for the amount needed to keep the country solvent within its debt repayment obligations*) So, it's no wonder that between 2012/2016 governments, particularly those in Europe, decided to target big multinationals by branding them as the great tax dodgers of our time. However, it should be noted that there was, and still isn't, any great desire to penalise these companies. They've simply become convenient scapegoats for inefficient governments with reckless economic policies. They have used multinational corporations to deflect public attention away from their own failings in a bid to sway public opinion in favour of the useless politicians of the world. And guess what? We've all fallen for it hook line and sinker. In order to redress the balance of knowledge, here is a brief synopsis of how we've been hoodwinked yet again.

As we've already discussed, major corporations come into existence with the financial muscle of collective investors. The money of investors is placed into a corporate pot and risked on the future of a particular enterprise. In return investors are legally entitled to a share of the profits in the event of future success but, they also have to risk total loss of their investment if all goes badly. Now, as any good accountant will tell you, all profits earned by a company belong to the investors whose money was staked in the enterprise to begin with. Companies do not actually make a profit for themselves. They may retain some of the profits earned for future expansion and product development, but that money still rightfully belongs to investors. As the enterprise grows and prospers it creates jobs. In the case of the big multinationals, hundreds of thousands of jobs across the world. All those employees are paid salaries upon which governments levy income tax and national/social security contributions - the collection of which, in many cases, is the responsibility of those corporations (*unpaid tax collectors*). These companies also create goods and services which are sold to the consumer. Again, taxes are due to governments upon those sales. In Europe an average of 20% VAT is added to the price of goods which has to be legally accounted for by those corporations. Major multinationals also create a series of individual micro economies of their own. They are directly responsible for the maintenance and growth of other businesses. It starts with the suppliers and manufacturers of their respective products. It continues with companies established to distribute and retail the company's products. Then there are the ancillary companies that sell or rent properties, vehicles, packaging materials, office equipment and all the people they employ. Add to that the local authority taxes they pay and the price of social contributions they make to local communities and it will be seen that multinational corporations play a major role in the well-being of most economies. All of this comes from the income generated by these companies. What is left over is deemed profit upon which governments levy corporation tax. And here lies the bone of contention.

Because multinationals are large companies whose stocks and shares are traded publicly on international stock exchanges, they have an obligation to protect the interests of shareholders. Those shareholders are largely investment companies and pension funds who are charged with the responsibility of providing financial returns to ordinary savers and pensioners. Therefore, it is important that multinationals are seen to be providing those essential financial returns. Fortunately, many governments around the world have enacted legislation that makes it possible for major companies to minimise their corporate tax liabilities through the prudent arrangement of corporate tax structures. This is done in order to attract major companies to set up shop in particular countries so that those countries can reap the social benefits of job creation and the development of ancillary services and businesses. It is precisely these incentives that have encouraged multinationals to establish complex offshore corporate structures that result in the vast transference of profit from higher tax jurisdictions to lower or no tax jurisdictions. This allows them to distribute a higher percentage of their profits back to their shareholders. Now this is a very important facet of modern business life. If a major corporation is forced into paying higher corporation taxes, it simply reduces the profits that are attributable to the shareholders - maybe the very same people who risked their capital to bring these companies into existence in the first place. If the shareholders start seeing diminished returns on their investment, they retaliate by dumping their stocks and shares. This reduces the value of shares and can even cause a stock market crash. The inevitable consequence of diminished investor confidence in a particular company cannot be over emphasised. Public confidence is also diminished which means the consumer buys less of the company's products or services. This directly forces the company to cut back on the number of people they employ as production falls. All the ancillary companies also have to cut back, creating even higher levels of unemployment in the wider community. Company offices, warehouses and distribution centres are left abandoned as the company slides into oblivion. Meanwhile, governments face a problem. There is less tax money coming into the system. There are increasing social welfare benefits to pay out to all those people who have lost their jobs. Local authorities have reduced income and find it difficult to maintain public services. So, why have we not seen a sudden explosion in demand for corporate reform to ensure a massive reduction of the financial power that these companies hold?

The answer is, yet again, kidology and the need for governments to deflect attention away from their own incompetence at handling the economy. The truth is that no government in the world has any intention of bringing about the downfall of a major corporation through draconian tax measures. They know by closing so-called tax avoidance loopholes and forcing companies to pay higher levels of corporation tax, their respective economies will suffer all the consequences highlighted above. It just isn't going to happen, but it doesn't stop politicians from making all the right noises as a means of appeasing public opinion. Lets take, for example, the 2013 public enquiry into corporate tax affairs in the UK. This was little more than a public relations exercise to deflect public gaze from the incompetence of the UK government's handling of the economy and it all happened, conveniently, in the run-up of the disclosure of massive tax avoidance in Panama. The UK government seized the opportunity to get the public on side by openly accusing the big multinationals of being "morally corrupt" by not paying their fair share of taxes to the UK economy. They did this by dragging some ageing, windbag politician out of the House of Lords to head up a public enquiry - a politician who had absolutely no knowledge of corporate affairs. They then ordered the CEOs of some of the world's largest corporations to attend the committee hearing in front of the nation's TV cameras. Instead of thanking the CEOs for their valuable contributions to the economic well-being of the country, and for creating thousands of jobs, they subjected them to the most humiliating inquisition into how they had structured their tax affairs to minimise their liabilities to pay corporation tax. They accused them of moral failings. Now excuse me for asking the obvious, but when was the payment of any tax a "moral" obligation? Throughout the history of taxation anywhere in the world, payment of taxes has only ever been a "legal" obligation, so where does morality creep into the picture? Clearly, if the government felt that these major corporations had escaped their "legal" obligation, they were free to amend the laws of the land to change tax avoidance into tax evasion. But, of course, and for reasons already stated, no government would want to change their laws. They simply wouldn't want to be held publicly accountable for the consequences of such legislative changes. So, it was easier for the UK government to use humiliation and moral arguments to win public support. Essentially, the government blackmailed these companies into a form of mild submission. By tarnishing their names the public reacted by demanding multinationals pay more taxes. The term "Moral Obligation" became entrenched in the minds of the public. There was absolutely no suggestion that any of these companies had committed any crime or broken any tax laws. But that term, moral obligation, kept rearing its head in every political debate thereafter. The overall effect was a potential public boycott of the products these big companies offered. So, in order to avoid a potential loss of confidence and all the negative consequences that could entail, many of the companies decided to make a voluntary contribution to the UK tax coffers, most notably, Google's voluntary donation of 130 million pounds. The contributions were minuscule in the scheme of things, but it did suffice to temporarily subdue the public. Of course, that wasn't the end of the matter, at least in the UK. Things did eventually quieten down a little. However, there is now an emerging political will to try and change tax legislation so that large corporations can be forced to pay higher levels of taxation. But, the one thing that's holding back the legislative changes is that no government, not in Europe anyway, wants to act unilaterally in implementing such changes. Instead, almost all European countries want to agree universal changes across all jurisdictions. This is simply so that no single country will be able to provide economic sanctuary to those companies that may wish to conduct their affairs in a more tax-efficient manner. What the knock on effect in the wider economy will be, no-one knows, but it's almost certain that a Europe-Wide change in tax legislation will make Europe a highly undesirable place to set up shop, and I can predict that many major corporations would rather relocate to a less zealous jurisdiction than suffer the dictatorial attitudes of a Europe that fully intends to gang-up on multinational corporations.

The financial system and its deficiencies has had a direct impact on all of us, even at very basic levels.

Take, for example, pension schemes. Technically speaking, these should be operated like savings pots that we each contribute to and have professionally managed for growth so that we all have a reasonable income during our retirement. In many respects, this is exactly what happens. However, there have been a lot of changes to the way pension schemes are managed and utilised over the years. Nowadays, most pension schemes are established as corporate schemes, thereby relieving governments of the obligation to provide us with a good standard of income during our retirement years. Although there is nothing fundamentally wrong with the concept, the practice has been far from satisfactory.   I remember when company pension schemes were first introduced into the UK. To my shock, I discovered that pension funds were offering some serious commission payments to so-called independent financial advisors for signing up companies into these schemes. The amount of commission was, in many cases, the equivalent of two years of contributions for every scheme established. This meant that the pension pots would be empty for at least two years of the scheme becoming operative. Furthermore, the pension companies were also applying management and administration costs to the funds, which accumulated even during the period in which the pension companies were recovering their commission payouts. Although there have been many pension reforms since those early days, designed to protect contributors in the event of company insolvency, there is still a possibility of pensioners getting short-changed. This happens when a government-established authority takes over the assets of pension scheme during company insolvency. It's usually the pensioners who take a hit for any shortfall in the pension assets. We saw this in 2016 when UK company BHS became insolvent. The previous owner of the company had sold BHS to a former bankrupt, Dominic Chappell for £1 in 2015. As such, the pension fund took a hit to an estimated £700 million. The previous owner, Sir Philip Green was eventually coerced into contributing some £363 million of his own money to help cover the deficit. This happened because during Chappell's period of ownership, Sir Philip Green, his family and other shareholders collected an estimated £580 million from BHS in dividends, rental payments and interest on loans. A parliamentary investigation subsequently declared that the company had been systematically plundered by its owners and called it "the unacceptable face of capitalism". State pensions schemes are also a travesty. Under these types of scheme, every employee and employer pays money to the government through compulsory national insurance or social security contributions. However, unlike with the corporate pension schemes, these contributions are not independently managed for growth by a pension fund. Instead they get lumped together with all the tax revenues collected by governments each year and are utilised for dealing with the demands of the economy as a whole. Given that most Western governments are up to their eyeballs in a sea of ever spiralling debt, there is very little chance of State pensions keeping pace with the needs of ageing populations. In fact, today's contributors are actually paying the pensions of yesterday's contributors. In any other sphere of commercial life, this would be classified as a "Ponzi Scheme" for which the law imposes very severe penalties.

At a more basic level, many people are totally unaware that they are being conned into maintaining the lifestyles of those involved in the regulated financial services sector. The one thing governments do not want to see is the financial sector get itself into trouble. They know that by encouraging them to keep creating consumer loans, we will all be able to continue buying stuff we don't need. That will keep the economy ticking over until an act of divine intervention sorts out our monetary problems. Such encouragement has seen the unfettered growth of credit card issuers, payday loan companies and in-store consumer credit companies. Payday loan companies often charge in excess of 1,000 percent APR, whilst credit card companies charge circa 21.8% APR. As for in store consumer credit, an average deal can see the price of consumer goods increase two fold on a typical 3 year credit deal. And, all this at a time when interest rates are supposed to be at an all-time low. So, while the financial services sector is fleecing consumers with exorbitant rates of interest on loans, the banks are actually charging us a fee for keeping our money in the bank. Unauthorised overdrafts of bank accounts is also another area of concern, so much so that in April 2017 a Treasury Select Committee in the UK tabled a motion to cap excessive charges made by banks. These charges generate £1.2 billion per annum for UK banks. For their part, the banks have been largely responsible for creating these charges. Essentially, a bank can see an account approaching a zero balance and decide to arbitrarily impose its monthly or quarterly bank charges on the account. This leads to accounts showing an unauthorised overdraft for which the bank can charge up to 90% interest for 28 days. It gets worse if the bank decides to inform you by letter, or asks you to visit your branch to give an explanation. Letters and visits often create additional charges which are added to your already overdrawn account. This, in itself, is yet more proof that banks don't actually lend money - they simply create money through the creation of debt. Think about it, they can simply plunge you into a debt obligation by imposing a charge on your account that you've never had the benefit of spending - the money simply never existed in the first place, but they expect you to pay back with real-world wonder-wallet-filler. This may all seem rather small in the scheme of things, but when you look at the statistics from a wider perspective, it isn't difficult to see what's going on in most Western economies. The average salary for a full-time employee in the UK (2014) was £27,195. By 2017, with pay rises capped by government, the average household consumer debt was close on £13,000 - and that doesn't include longer term mortgage debt. What is really worrying is that this debt level is steadily increasing at a rate of about 6% per year. All this debt amounted to a whopping £1.5 trillion in 2016. So, its easy to see what the game is here. Get as much of the circulating cash back into the financial services sector as fast as possible so they have the cash assets to add to their balance sheets so they can keep on creating more and more new money. The more money they create, the more they can lend you at high rates of interest so that you can keep the economy going by spending way beyond your financial means. Its a disaster just waiting to happen.

When trying to predict how the new revolutionaries are going to solve the massive, global problem of the financial system, we can only conclude that it will involve "financial abstinence". It's the only remedy for this major issue we are all facing. Essentially, people will simply stop spending on garbage products or services that we are constantly bombarded with through ever-increasing volumes of advertising - we simply won't have the incomes to support the required borrowing. Our revolutionaries will wake up to the fact that buying every new gadget or gizmo just because we will be considered social outcasts if we don't have them, is sheer lunacy. They will start to stay at home, cook food instead of ordering junk takeaways. They'll cancel their pay entertainment subscriptions and watch free-to-air channels instead. They'll stick with last year's model of smartphone or flat-screen TV and they will stop buying video games to play on their expensive game consoles. They may decide to keep their domestic appliances, cars and furniture for a few more years instead of trashing them all because there is a new "toy" on the market. The bottom line effect will be that the revolutionaries will stop borrowing money. That would be a real wake up call for governments. If people stopped borrowing and lived within their means, even if only for a few years, most Western economies will tank. The reduction in money supply will take us back to the financial crisis we experienced in 2007/2008. That will be the catalyst for real change to the whole monetary system. We almost got there during the last financial crisis, but if it happens again in the near future and it hits harder than before, there will be hope for us all. Only by forcing politicians into a corner will we be able to exert real change on a global basis.

The Rise of Technology

One of the main features of the modern world that will play a significant role in the next revolution is technology. The whole world seems to be interconnected with individuals who, for the first time ever, are able to communicate on a scale previously reserved for mainstream media and broadcasting companies. But, has this happened by accident or by design? It's a question we should be asking ourselves. When we look back at the rapid rise of technological influence on our lives, there are certain things that simply do not stack-up in the scheme of things. For the first time ever, the human race has voluntarily opened up their lives to scrutiny, firmly believing that they have a new-found freedom at their fingertips. But, is it freedom, or is it oppression? Have we become slaves to a sector of society who would use technology to control, snoop and share information about every facet of our lives? To better understand the rationale behind my questions, lets take a sneak-peek back in time to see where it all started.

The concept of the Internet in the form of the World Wide Web was invented by Tim-Berners Lee, a British computer scientist in the 1980's. However, much of the technological development of the Internet started way before then in the 1950's, primarily for use by the military. Much of the early development took place during the 1960's in the USA at the University of California and the Stanford Research Institute. However, it was the development of the World Wide Web that really brought the Internet to ordinary people around the world. Since the mid 1990's, the World Wide Web has revolutionised the way people communicate. Its impact has been felt on our cultures, commerce and other areas of normal day to day life generally. Of course, all this communication capability would be of little use to us mere mortals had it not been for the invention of the Personal Computer. Whilst there had been many predecessors to the personal computer we know today, it wasn't until IBM first launched its Personal Computer in 1981, that the real impact of global communications by ordinary people started to take off.

It was also when IBM introduced its Personal Computer that we saw a major shift in commercial attitudes towards technology development. Prior to the IBM launch, almost all manufacturers would have gone out of their way and spent considerable amounts of money protecting their inventions from imitations. Not so with IBM. When they introduced their Personal Computer it brought with it a new terminology called "Open Architecture". This meant that all manner of third-party components and add-ons could be manufactured by anyone in the world. IBM actively encouraged PC owners to open up their computer boxes and stuff them with all sorts of bolt-ons and extras that would enable the computer itself to perform a wide range of other tasks, including communications using ordinary telephone lines. This is when the World Wide Web really took-off for most people. It was also the point where personal computing started to become affordable. Although a medium power IBM PC would have set you back about 3,000 dollars back in the 1980's, The rise in manufacturing of third party components and even complete clones of the IBM Personal Computer in the Far East resulted in a rapid decrease of prices, making the personal computer accessible to just about everyone. In order for these new personal computers to become popular with the masses, they had to be simple to use. That's when Microsoft first stepped into the picture. A fresh-faced Bill Gates, straight out of high school was awarded the opportunity by IBM to develop the PC-DOS operating system (*latterly to become MS-DOS and ultimately the Windows operating system that much of the world uses today*). This allowed people to interact with an otherwise complex piece of technology by tapping graphical icons on screen with a pointing device known as a Mouse. This made personal computers far more intuitive, to the point where no-one needed any technical knowledge to use one. This ultimately led to eye-watering amounts of investment into new technology and software companies that could fuel the inevitable appetite for consumer-driven products and applications. One such company was the mighty Google who dominate the search engine market, making it simple for users to find all manner of information on the rapidly expanding World Wide Web. Again, this was a company founded by a fresh-faced kid just out of high-school. While other companies who had been around longer, such as Netscape, Yahoo and a few others, simply couldn't stop the rise of Google with its huge investment backing.

Now, at this point, we should perhaps go back to those searching questions we raised earlier, only this time we should delve a little deeper. Why did a major US computer manufacturer suddenly develop a product which was open for all to copy? Most people would assume that by protecting the intellectual property that went into the IBM PC, the company could have maintained a global dominance of the PC market. But, this would not necessarily have seen the explosive growth in technology acceptance in the consumer market. So, it appears that someone, somewhere wanted this explosive growth in connecting the world. The only way that could be realistically achieved was by opening up the market to lower priced competitors the world over. The upside of course, at least for the USA, was that Silicon Valley took off big time and the mighty Microsoft were handed a global market for operating systems on a plate. Every PC manufacturer in the world would have to pay Microsoft a licence fee to pre-install a copy of the Windows Operating System on every PC manufactured. Then there was the massive investment into companies like Microsoft and Google. Who instigated that? And, were governments in any way behind this massive technology investment? Was there an agenda to positively encourage the world to become so interconnected? Were deals done with these technology giants to ensure that ordinary people could be snooped upon without them ever being aware of what was happening? Think about it. If governments gave everyone a free Personal Computer and told them to use it they have to put all their personal life details on line for all to see, would the idea have ever caught on? I doubt it. But, by leading us all into believing that we could now empower ourselves by purchasing low-cost technology from commercial organisations that would enrich our lives, we all bought into the idea. What appears to have happened is that Governments actively wanted us exposed to privacy exploitation and got us to pay for it by creating a massive industry that could promote all the advantages of using technology in our every day lives, but leaving us largely oblivious to the fact that our interconnectivity could be used for more sinister purposes.

Having got many of the world's homes and offices connected to an information highway, the next step was to get individuals connected, thus breaking down the distribution of personal information to individual people, rather than just their homes and places of work. This came about with the development of the mobile phone. Prior to 2007, many mobile phones were just that, a device for making phone calls on the move. Some could also send simple text messages. Some manufacturers also started developing extended functionality such as the ability to send and receive email, browsing the internet and giving access to a limited range of basic applications such as a calculator or an appointment scheduler. Companies such as Sony used a new operating system called Symbian, others, notably Blackberry, developed proprietary operating systems that could only work on their specific devices. Needless to say, wide acceptance was slow, with only Blackberry becoming dominant in the corporate markets. Then, in 2007, the world was introduced to the iPhone, developed by Apple. This was a real smartphone that used only touch-screen technology and screen icons to make the phone do everything it was capable of. It was a fantastic device which was so intuitive, it didn't even need an instruction manual. Its one button would fire the device into action with all its other functions being just a screen-tap away. There were no fiddly set-up routines, just turn it on and you were good to go.

Now came a big problem. Apple used proprietary technology and software to drive its smartphone. The operating system could not be used on any other device and Apple were not willing to licence it to other manufacturers. Therefore, consumers who wanted the iPhone's level of design and functionality would have to shell out quite a substantial amount of money to buy the device. Of course, that in itself didn't stop the iPhone from becoming the best selling Smartphone at the time. However, the sale of the iPhone was restricted to those who could afford it. Clearly, this wasn't going to help in the mass acceptance of a world of individuals all connected and identifiable by the fingerprints left by smartphone technology. Something had to be done. A new revolution in technology had to happen, a revolution that would give consumers all the functionality and simplicity of the iPhone at a price that everyone could afford. Say hello to Android (*now part of Google*). This new operating system had the ability to match all the features that Apple's iPhone could offer, but could be licensed to any manufacturer for inclusion into their smartphone offerings. The first Android driven smartphone was eventually released in 2008 by HTC. Although it didn't look much like the iPhone, it did have the graphical user interface that the world wanted. Soon after, other manufacturers started releasing iPhone lookalikes, but being very careful not to infringe Apple's one-button design patents. Soon, the world was littered with low-cost smartphones. Just like in the earlier PC market, the smartphone was now available to everyone at a price we could all afford. To encourage market growth in smartphone usage, telecommunications providers leapt into action with low cost sim cards and usage plans that would ensure the whole world could afford to be connected. The end result is that we have all become totally exposed to everyone in the world who may wish to exploit us as individuals. Nowhere has this been more so than in the explosive growth of social networks such as Facebook. Through social networks, individuals expose every facet of their lives to the outside world. They share everything from what they are having for dinner, to their latest sexual encounters. They fill their social network accounts with images of themselves, their families and everyone else they may encounter in their everyday lives. Never has so much personal data been available to anyone who has the cash to pay for it.

This massive personal exposure to the world at large should give us cause for concern. Not only because commercial organisations can use the information to sell you things directly, but because we don't really know if some of these technology giants have cut a deal with government agencies that exposes you to all sorts of potential investigations. Having worked in the financial services arena for many years, I know first hand how damaging social networks can be. There are organisations all over the world that are paid by companies to check out the status of prospective employees. They scour the internet and social networks to find out who you are, where you hang out, what your likes and dislikes are and who your personal and professional associates are. Just think about this for a while. If you were at a social event that was also attended by a notorious crook, it only needs that crook, or someone else at the event to snap a picture of the two of you together and post it online somewhere to raise the alarm bells if there was a subsequent investigation into the crook's activities. If you were applying for an important job in say the financial services sector, the chances are that if your picture is somewhere on line, it will be the focus of further investigation. If you are seen in the company of unsavoury people, whether you knew it or not, you will automatically be branded as someone with questionable associates. You may not even be told that this research is being undertaken, but for sure it is and your ability to get a better job could be seriously impaired. The sad thing is you won't even know the reason why. Then there is the question of police investigations. Once investigators start scouring the social network pages of undesirables, you may well be one of those unfortunates who get targeted for further investigation simply by association.

Social media has also been responsible for the growing animosity we see in the world today. The ability of ordinary people to make their voices heard (*often anonymously*) has given rise to a complete breakdown in empathy towards others and our ability to communicate sensibly. We've witnessed young children being driven to take their own lives because of the nastiness of other children who feel it's ok to broadcast the most hideous things without any fear of being found out. We've seen trouble makers use the Internet to spread false allegations and to exploit the vulnerabilities of their fellow man. We've seen people driven out of business through spiteful competitors posting false reviews on line, and we've seen the mass sexual exploitation of young people through online grooming. The problem is, no one seems to care. Nothing seems to get done to prevent this online abuse. It's no wonder really, given that most politicians actually want to use the Internet and social media themselves. They use these tools to get their personal political messages across to us on a one to one basis. They want nothing to do with controlling or regulating the Internet or the social networks that use this medium. One only has to look at politicians seated in their respective parliaments to see how they are exploiting the situation. Every day, we see them using smartphones to tweet their latest propaganda to the masses instead of doing the job they are paid to do. Social media has also aided the mass exploitation of migrants fleeing from places like Syria. Many of these people are being led by a relatively small group of their fellow countrymen who have access to smartphones and tablet devices. These people research where they want to end up, to find those countries that will give migrants the best possible social assistance. They then charge thousands of dollars or Euros to lead groups of migrants on a journey that can often result in death at sea. When they do eventually arrive on the shores of a European country, they stir up trouble by breaking down border fences in an endeavour to make it to their preferred destination. They exploit the frustrations of those genuinely needy migrants who may not understand the language or the culturally acceptable behaviour of the countries they arrive in. As such, they are easily encouraged to form themselves into a marauding mass of uncontrollable people who will stop at nothing to reach their preferred destination.

Of course, Whilst this mass exploitation of people's misery is going on, Western politicians weigh-in on the debate by accusing some European countries of not doing enough to help fleeing migrants. I even watched a televised political debate in the UK in which politicians were attempting to shame the UK government into doing more by comparing the UK's willingness to help the Jews fleeing Nazi controlled Europe during World War II while doing very little to help the Syrian migrants. Of course, what they forgot to mention is that many unoccupied European countries actually gave sanctuary to the persecuted Jews with open arms. In many cases, we even helped them to escape. The reason being that those seeking sanctuary were actually grateful for the help they received. Many of them settled and made valuable contributions to the societies they found themselves in. Unlike the modern migrants that attempt to enter Europe, the Jewish community didn't come armed with Smartphones, demanding settlement in a particular country. They understood that the people who were offing help were not in a financial position to offer much more than shelter and the sharing of scarce food resources.

Compare that with the migrants who ended up on the beaches of Greece. Instead of accepting whatever hospitality the Greeks could offer and wait for the government to process their asylum applications in an orderly manner, they were incited into breaking free so that they could find their own way to countries that they felt could give them something better.

Social media and all the technology that surrounds it has also been used for misinforming people about events around the world. If you looked at many Russian social media sites during the Ukrainian civil war of 2014, they were littered with cruel and hateful comments about the situation in Ukraine. Whilst the initial propaganda was fuelled by state controlled media within Russia, the stories got accentuated and spread like wild fire through social networks. If many of these stories were to be believed, we would have to believe that Ukrainians were eating Russian babies for breakfast. The fact is, they were all one people in the not too distant past, and yet, the rise of fast and fake news led to huge animosity between these countries and all because of social media networks. When the Malaysian airliner was shot down over Ukraine during the height of the civil war, social media came to the fore again. This time it was to start spreading the various theories and "so called" facts about what happened and who was responsible. There were so many different versions of events that the vast majority of them had to be lies - they couldn't all be right. And so, mass hysteria was provoked yet again by an uncontrolled mass of false information being fed to the world by people who, in many cases, were not even there or qualified to give an opinion. This was all an added bonus for the Russian Government, but did very little to bring comfort or closure to those families who's lives had been devastated by the incident.

Even in our every day lives, we seem to have lost the ability to engage in the most basic of conversations. You can sit in restaurants and watch as people engage in conversation through the use of a smartphone. They could be talking to each other or to people who are not in the restaurant - who knows. People can often be seen wandering around busy streets firmly plugged into their devices and engaging in online chats with other people. They bump into things and other pedestrians, in some cases they even walk out into traffic, completely oblivious to the fact that they stand a very good chance of being killed by an oncoming vehicle. It's absolute madness and something we seem powerless to change. We've become zombies, so reliant upon the interconnected world that we forget we are basic human beings who were born with a natural ability to communicate with other human beings without being tied by a digital umbilical cord to a smart device.

The most worrying aspects of the "plugged-in" world we live in is that we have inadvertently become the first line of a supply chain which makes multi-billionaires out of relatively young people. This is leading to a mass overvaluation of technology companies which we are then encouraged to invest into. It's unbelievable that some of these companies can make no profits (*in some cases they make hundreds of millions in losses*) and then be valued at billions of dollars at the point where the original investors want pay-back with inflated profits. Because we all believe these companies are worth the money, we go flocking to the stock exchanges to buy up shares during the initial public offering. What happens thereafter is all down to luck and the mood of the markets, but the fact remains that the public sale of shares in these companies make their founders and initial shareholders seriously wealthy. This has been one of the chief factors in the creation of unequal societies. The transference of wealth from the masses to a handful of fortunate business people has helped create inequalities across the board. As the rich get richer, the poor get poorer. The sad truth is it doesn't end there. As more and more of these technology companies become entrenched with information about each and every one of us, they sell this information on to other wealthy enterprises who use it to target us into buying things that we may not ordinarily buy. Not only do we get targeted, we get absolutely bombarded. If you buy something on Amazon or eBay, for sure you will receive a string of emails telling you that other people who bought the product also bought this, that or the other product. It's almost like brainwashing us into believing that we will somehow become social outcasts if we don't also buy the same things. It's compelling marketing that really only serves to bolster the consumer society that governments crave. They need us to keep buying as a means of boosting the economy and we fall for it every time. Another worrying aspect is the fact that you, as an individual, can be precisely pinpointed and located almost anywhere on the planet. This gives commercial organisations and government agencies an immense amount of power. They can discover where you've been, who you were talking to, how much time you spent at a particular location and, particularly useful for the criminal fraternity, how long you have been away from your home. Criminals are also obtaining the ability to hack into your connected systems. Smartphones are often used to monitor your home and its appliances while you are away. How easy would it be for a criminal to hack into your security system and turn it off? For sure, a determined criminal can discover when you are out and about, so it's only a matter of time before that knowledge can be used to target your home for a bit of good old-fashioned burglary. If you doubt my words, take this as an example. I was in a restaurant in Bucharest where I enjoyed a very nice meal in the company of friends. Upon arriving back at our hotel, each of us received a message from Google. The message displayed a small map highlighting the precise location of the restaurant, the time we were there and asking us to write a review of the restaurant so that other Google users could read our views of the establishment. If this type of information and intrusion into our lives can be undertaken for commercial marketing, for sure it can be used by government agencies or criminals who have the technical know how to use these features. It isn't without reason that governments the world over have invested into huge data collection centres to collect information about emails text and voice messages being sent across the world. They go to great lengths to tell us that the information gathered doesn't personally identify the individual so we have to ask the question, why bother to collect the information if there is no way to use it for identifying a potential criminal? If a restaurant in Bucharest can pay Google to track its customers and solicit a review from them, then other, non-commercial organisations and criminals can do the same. Furthermore, this highlights how the likes of Google use us to make billions of dollars every year. They fool us into offering personal data to them free of charge so that they can sell that information on for a profit to anyone who has the money to pay for it.

The information being tracked is increasing by the day. If you have a "wearable" such as a smart watch, or one of those health tracking wrist bands, companies can find out a lot about you as a person. They can see how fit and healthy you are. They know if you exercise regularly. They can see how many steps you've walked, jogged or run in a particular day. They can even monitor your heartbeat and blood pressure, all because you've been persuaded to buy a simple device that connects to your smartphone or tablet. At a more sinister level, you could be engaged in a secret affair, or maybe you are leaving a digital trail of places you've visited that others may think are a little unsavoury. For example, you could be tracked visiting a local bar where you spend a few hours with friends. You then use your smart payment system on your phone to pay the bill. Next, you go off to a sleazy nightclub where you spend a few more hours and end the night with a very large bill which you also pay using your smart payment system. Now, someone, somewhere knows that you've spent the evening knocking back a few drinks and that you've been to a club where, judging by the size of your payment, you may well have engaged with a lady of the night (*this could also be confirmed by your heart rate monitor that's firmly attached to your wrist*). Whilst this may not be the best behaviour to condone, do you really want that private data being used by others to target you in some way or another? I guess not. It may even reach a point where a clever hacker gets hold of that data and uses it to blackmail you against the threat of having your night-time antics revealed on a social network for the whole world to see. It's not beyond the realms of possibility. The more we voluntarily sign-up to all this digital technology, the more likely it is to come back and bite us on the butt in the future. We've already seen the mass hacking of major computer systems, both corporate and governmental. These hacks have highlighted the very real dangers of getting more deeply entrenched into the connected digital world and yet we all seem to crave more and more intrusions into our lives. It's time we woke up to what we're doing and start taking steps to minimise our exposure. When the next revolution starts to manifest itself, there will be a great reliance on technology to rally support among the masses. However, that support can be easily thwarted if government agencies think it could give rise to anarchy. It can also be used to identify those who would seek to change the status quo. Therefore, one of the first priorities of the new revolutionaries will be to find ways to disconnect from the personal information gathering and tracking that the modern world has thrown at us, and find ways to keep the communication stream flowing in a more private environment. It won't be an easy task, but one that will have to come about if a total breakdown of normal human communication is to be avoided. People will eventually realise how their lives are being totally controlled by major global corporations, government agencies and the criminal fraternity. They will understand that all this cheap technology hasn't been thrown at us to enhance our lives, but instead it's there to increase the fortunes of a few major companies whilst giving governments increased powers of control over everything we do. In the scheme of things, we are only a short step away from total surrender, so we must start thinking logically again.

When it comes to the rise of the big multi-nationals, particularly those engaged in the technology sector, there is nothing intrinsically wrong with their size or the products they produce. The problem has more to do with the way in which their products are used to increasingly gather information about us and then selling it on to the highest bidder. As I mentioned in the chapter about economics, there is nothing wrong with companies becoming big. They do, after all, create jobs that do help economies grow by allowing their employees to earn income upon which they pay taxes. Furthermore, the VAT and sales taxes levied upon the products and services supplied by these companies goes some considerable way to reducing tax burdens on ordinary citizens. Where I do see a problem is in the vast false wealth created for the founders and the founding shareholders and the minimal growth opportunities afforded to secondary investors (*you and I*) into the technology sector. Obviously, it would be foolish to simply ignore the contribution made by founders and initial investors in the establishment of these corporations in the first place. The founders and their initial shareholders should rightly be rewarded for the risks they took in the early years of company development. But, it appears to have got completely out of hand in the technology sector. As I've stated above, the problem stems from the fact that during an IPO, the companies are grossly overvalued by the financial and banking sector. This is often driven by pure greed and the need to make a secondary market that can be manipulated by the investment sector. It also sees a massive shift of money from one sector of society (*savers and small investors*) into the hands of a few people who originally started the company. Those people are then free to walk away with huge amounts of money that has never actually been earned, neither does it have to be returned to anyone. What happens thereafter is a simple game. Essentially, those who control the investment markets engage in buy and sell activities between themselves. None of the proceeds of these transactions really affect or benefit the companies whose stocks and shares are being traded. Instead it's a simple question of every dollar lost by one investor on a secondary sale, is a dollar profit for another investor. The markets can, therefore, be manipulated by institutional investors by taking out buy or sell orders at a future value, then buying or selling their shares to force prices in the direction they wish them to go in order to realise a profit on their future transactions. It's this buying and selling activity that moves share prices. When a lot of investors are selling, the price goes down. When there are more buyers than sellers, the price goes up. So all that's happening in the stock markets is groups of traders buying and selling to each other, Some make money, some lose money, but ultimately, nothing gets created of any real tangible value. Of course, over time, and depending upon the distributable profits earned by companies, share prices can also rise in value further due to the increasing attractiveness of higher earning shares and the consequent buying demand for them. This is another form of kidology. Most of us believe that if share prices tumble, it's all to do with company performance. The fact is, it's all to do with the perceived value of the company when something negative happens within the company. Technology businesses are very susceptible to this type of value fluctuation. We've seen it with Facebook, SnapChat and even big technology manufacturers like Samsung. It only needs a product to go bad, or profits to take a downturn to cause loss of investor confidence. This alone can trigger a share selling spree that leaves ordinary investors with huge losses. The strange thing is, once those losses have been realised, other investors snap up the shares to make even larger gains when the immediate corporate problems are solved.

Our increasing thirst for even more technology products is going to see even more fortunes being made by technology companies across the spectrum. We, as consumers, will undoubtedly just go with the flow with little regard to the knock-on consequences of embracing every new innovation that comes along. Take, for example, the driverless car. This will create a huge conundrum for governments around the world. Questions will have to be asked such as, will there continue to be a need for driving licences and driving tuition and tests? Will the responsibility of insurance fall to the technology companies who are, in effect, driving our vehicles? Will we be responsible for traffic offences committed by our vehicles? Whatever the answers, it will be the consumer who will end up footing the bill. Governments make money when they sell you a driving licence. The economy would suffer if all the driving schools and test centres were to be disbanded, and insurance companies would see a huge decrease in premium income. The reduced persecution of drivers through the imposition of traffic fines would certainly leave a big hole in government revenues. The possibility exists that we will either pay a huge premium for the privilege of owning a driverless car to compensate for all this lost revenue, or, as I suspect, we will still have to follow existing rules that oblige us to have a driving license, sit a test, have lessons, buy insurance and still be responsible for the payment of traffic fines even though we will be mere passengers in a vehicle being driven by a computer. You see, wherever new innovation results in a reduction of revenues for other sectors, it will always be the consumer who foots the bill. To understand just how gullible we have all become, we only have to look at the number of people that still buy travel insurance. Think about it, what are you being covered for. Medical expenses while you are travelling abroad, loss of limbs or life as a result of an accident while travelling, lost baggage, and flight delays. For many travellers, such insurance is totally unnecessary. In Europe, for example, medical expenses are usually covered by your own national health provider. Air disasters resulting in serious injury or loss of life are covered by the airline's insurance. Lost baggage is also compensated for by the airlines. Under European regulations, airlines are now obliged to compensate you for extended flight delays. So all those premiums that many people throw at a travel insurance are just a waste of money. The same thing will happen with the introduction of driverless vehicles. We will all be conned into buying all sorts of unnecessary insurance products in order to satisfy the law, but we are unlikely to ever claim on those policies. This is why I have my doubts as to whether we will see totally driverless cars. I can foresee a pact being entered into by the technology companies and governments that ensures that there is always going to be a manual override in driverless vehicles, even if it is never used, in order to maintain the requirement for licences, tests, tuition and insurance whilst still making us all responsible for the actions of the vehicle even when it's in driverless mode. This will keep the traffic fines and other revenues pouring in, whilst reducing the actual expenditures, particularly for insurers. I can well foresee a day when traffic cops will be replaced with digital data being fed from the vehicle to regulatory authorities who will simply fine us through the post for a whole raft of new offences dreamed up specifically for driverless car owners. We already see this in the use of digital speed cameras on our roads. One snap and, hey presto!, an almost instant speeding fine drops in your mailbox complete with a picture of your vehicle, it's registration number and, in some countries, a clear image of the driver and front-seat passenger (*that can be the cause of problems far worse than a traffic fine*).

So, before we fully embrace the constant stream of new technologies being bestowed upon us, we should, perhaps, take a step back and think a little more about what it's really going to do to our lives. We should ask ourselves what the true cost will be. We all have choices and we can prevent ourselves from being, literally, taken for a ride. The next revolutionaries will undoubtedly have something to say about new technologies and will inevitably make concerted efforts to minimise the impact on the lives of ordinary people. Already, some visionaries of the world have understood what this rapid advancement of technology will hold for us all. We know now that technology has been responsible for a huge reduction in employment levels. It's all very well saying that the younger generation will just have to find employment in the technology sector, but there isn't any real masterplan to ensure a painless transition. If our driverless world really takes off I can foresee thousands of cab drivers losing their jobs. We already see driverless transport systems ferrying passengers between terminals at major airports. How long will it be before that idea finds its way to the wider public transport systems? Driverless trains and busses are certainly on the way. Our manufacturing sector is now flooded with huge robots that have taken the place of real people. We have package and postal deliveries being undertaken by drones and robots. Our streets are being policed with surveillance cameras instead of real police officers. We order our weekly shop online and wait for it to be despatched from huge computer operated distribution centres. What we are likely to end up with is increasing poverty as there will be fewer employment opportunities. And, all this is happening while the world's population is increasing at an alarming rate. Ordinary people will be consigned to the trashcan of employment history, relying increasingly upon government handouts to sustain a basic level of survival. Some visionaries have even suggested the ultimate solution. They envision a world comprised of self-sufficient towns and cities that provide housing, food, transport, education, healthcare and power generation for its citizens. Money will disappear as it will simply become an obstacle to progress. Instead, every citizen will be expected to contribute to the operation of the city by working to keep the whole technology-focused infrastructure working. But, wait a minute! isn't that what communism was supposed to be? Remember those poor Russians in the former USSR. They got given everything they needed in their lives, but had to devote themselves to working for the State. Surely, that can't be the model that our Western democracies have in store for us! Or maybe it is, but maybe they don't want to enlighten us just yet. For sure, something has to break before things can improve. We are currently all hovering our fingers over a great big self-destruct button so, we have to start waking up soon. Hopefully, the next revolution will start a major rethink of how our futures will be moulded for the better. It won't be easy and it will take a huge amount of political will. The problem is, politicians and the mega wealthy they support will never let go of the powers they currently enjoy. So the revolutionary tactics employed may well have to be drastic. We should be prepared for such drastic action by making our voices heard before the crap hits the fan.

My own personal take on the technology factor is that the plans are very simple. Economic devaluation of human beings. Basically, a world is currently being planned, mainly by technology companies, where human beings will have absolutely no economic value unless they are gainfully employed creating even more technology products. This is going to cause a major problem for governments all over the world. What do you do with all those economically redundant citizens? Do you simply give them sufficient money to buy homes, feed themselves and have a little left over to have some fun with, or do you push them to one side and leave them to fend for themselves? It's a big question that needs a reassuring answer fairly quickly. If the answer isn't built into the long term plan, then the resulting revolution may well be bloody and violent. The best we can hope for is that our politicians have given it some thought and maybe have a few tricks up their sleeves to save the world from an otherwise messy meltdown. It's wishful thinking, I know. I've yet to come across any politician who can think beyond their term of office, let alone think what sort of world they are helping to create for future generations. Our best hope is that some early revolutionaries will start asking more pointed questions of our candidate politicians before voting them into a position of power.

The Terrorism Factor

In recent years the world as a whole, and more particularly in Europe, has witnessed a dramatic rise in terrorism that targets ordinary people. These sickening acts of violence often target people who are doing little more then getting on with their normal way of life. We've seen the mass killing of citizens in France, the UK, Germany, the USA and even as far afield as Australia. Acts of terror, of course, are not a new thing. Back in the days of the Irish Republican Army (*the IRA*), it was relatively simple for terrorists groups to pinpoint disenfranchised Irish people living in mainland UK and persuade them to commit atrocious acts of violence against ordinary British citizens within their own country. Some of the most brazen attacks were the bombings in Birmingham, Brighton and Manchester. Now it has to be said, just like modern day terrorist groups, the atrocities committed by the relatively small number of extremists doesn't always meet with the approval of supporters of the organisations in who's names the acts are committed in the first place. A prime example of this was the massive fundraising that went on in the USA on behalf of the IRA. Many American contributors to the fund raising effort actually believed they were helping a quasi-political group reach their goals in a reasonably civilised and democratic manner. The reality was that all that American money was being diverted into bomb-making factories and weapons acquisition which would have a deadly impact on innocent people in mainland Britain.

In recent times, terrorism has become an increasingly urgent problem. It's hardly surprising when you start to look deeper at what we in the West have done to alienate so many people around the world. We've got involved in other people's affairs, we've invaded countries for no other reason than to implement regime-change, often toppling and executing the dictatorships that once kept these countries and regions under control. The problem is we've then walked away and left these countries to their own devices, many of whom have several factions that are waiting to fill the power vacuum. We've essentially left the foxes in charge of the chicken run. This has resulted in civil wars which have ultimately led to masses of migrants seeking sanctuary in other countries. Those migrants, although initially grateful for any help they receive, quickly become angry and bitter towards the West for the interference in their lives. Their once tolerable lifestyle, even under a dictatorship was, in their opinion, far better than the resulting carnage caused by internal power struggles within their respective countries.

Europe has been particularly vulnerable to the plight of migrants from places like Syria and North African countries. France in particular has always had a close affinity with North African States and many migrants from that region have always had an automatic right to enter France and become French citizens. The UK also had similar arrangements with the commonwealth countries over which they once ruled. Whilst this migration was well intentioned and controlled in the past, such as for the rebuilding of the UK after the devastating effects of World War II, in more recent times, its become a mechanism that has had a serious impact on the demographics of countries like the UK, France, Holland and Germany. In the past, mass migration has generally been good for the economies who opened up their doors to migrant workers. Many people who entered the UK from places like India, Africa, Pakistan, Asia etc. felt they were seizing an opportunity to change their lives and those of their families. It was a two-way street that benefitted everyone. The UK, for example, needed to rebuild the economy and replenish it's depleted labour-force. The immigrants that came to help the UK achieve this were guaranteed jobs for themselves, healthcare and an education for their children. It was a perfect partnership. The same was probably true in France and Germany. But, in more recent times, the migrant populations of many European countries, including those family members that were actually born in the host country, have become disenfranchised from mainstream society. They have been forced into ghettos on the outskirts of major centres of population. Many are finding it increasingly difficult to find jobs and rely heavily on government subsidies in order to survive. Society in general has left them out in the cold and in many cases, they've become forgotten by governments. Opportunities and education are diminishing, leaving a whole new generation of family members to fend for themselves in an increasingly harsh social environment. This is a pattern that is emerging across Europe and is leading to radicalisation of some members of the migrant communities. These are angry people who feel they have been left out of society. The division between those that have and those that have not is widening by the day and at a rate that has never been seen before. Much of this has been brought about by the European Union and its quest to Europeanise everything across the continent. Its transferred vast wealth into specific sectors of society whilst leaving the less well off to fend for themselves. As in previous generations, governments will always seek to attack the poor as a means of shoring up economies. Labour is often exploited and the meagre salaries earned by the poorer members of society are often taxed at source so there can be no escaping the requirement to hand over a large part of your earnings to governments. To make matters even more unfair, the EU is harmonising the exchange of tax information across the continent. In many instances it's now almost impossible to undertake cross-border business without a formal declaration that an individual or a business has a fiscal tax residency. We are told this is to make for a fairer society in which everyone will make a fair contribution towards the cost of operating a federalised Europe. The reality is that it is often used to penalise ordinary people as they find themselves increasingly exposed to ever increasing demands for a bigger slice of their pay check. For the disenfranchised, this is an even bigger problem than we may give it credit for. Migrant workers in most western societies are among the most lowly paid people out there. They tend to do all those jobs that the mainstream don't want to do and become little more than part of a constant stream of cheap labour to do those jobs.   Even though these people are barely earning the minimum wage for basic survival, they still have to pay taxes to the government. So, it's easy to see how such people can be radicalised into committing acts of terrorism as a means of getting their voices heard in a world where inequalities between the wealthy and the poor are increasing at an alarming rate.

This, of course, is no excuse for committing an act of terrorism. Unfortunately, in some cultures, even in today's world, violent extremism is considered the norm for settling disputes - something our left wing politicians seem to forget when they insist on opening borders to even greater levels of immigration. The terrorist atrocities witnessed in Europe during 2016/2017 were committed by home grown extremists who were all legally resident in Europe. Furthermore, these people were free to travel across Schengen borders from one European country to another. This allowed them to commit an act of terrorism in one country and then flee to another country without detection or challenge. It's absolute madness and yet free movement of people is also a fundamental principle of EU membership. A similar situation was true of the 9/11 attacks in New York. Although the jury may still be out on what really happened on 9/11, the official line is that this atrocious act of terrorism was committed by a group of people who were all resident in the USA (*although at least six of them were in violation of their visa conditions*). It wasn't an act committed directly by a foreign power, it wasn't a missile launched from another country, it was a group of foreign nationals who had successfully and legally entered the USA. They then walked into their local airport, hijacked aircraft and took to the skies without anyone noticing. It was clearly the case that these people had been radicalised by a foreign organisation that was hell-bent on punishing the West for past actions or indiscretions. But, the resulting acts of terror were largely committed by individuals who gained legal entry into the USA and were sympathetic to a misguided cause.

Although the main aim of any act of terrorism is to cause death and destruction on a grand scale, it also has a wider impact on ordinary citizens - an impact that can cause a major erosion in the freedoms of millions of people world wide. It was author and conspiracy theorist, David Ike, that coined the expression Problem - Reaction - Solution. This was his take on how governments enforce ever increasing levels of control over the lives of ordinary citizens. It starts with a problem, normally a major act of terrorism, that jolts us all into a state of panic. The problem itself can be just a random, unplanned act of violence, or it can be a government instigated act. Whatever the act, the reaction kicks in. Ordinary citizens are so shocked by the problem they immediately demand their politicians do something about it. This leads to the solution which often means greater control over the lives of ordinary citizens. In the case of 9/11 the problem was clear and broadcast to the whole world on live TV. The immediate reaction from most of the world, and within the US was that something drastic had to be done. This was the catalyst that then president George W. Bush needed to implement a whole range of draconian measures that would change the lives of everyone world-wide. It wasn't the tragic loss of life that spurred Bush into action - it couldn't have been because more lives are lost on the roads of America every month than were lost in the 9/11 attacks. This, in no way, attempts to draw a comparison between acts of terror and accidental deaths on the roads of America. However, it does illustrate the anomaly of public reaction to mass deaths in a single incident and mass deaths occurring over a longer period of time. The same can be said of gun crime in the USA. It only takes a mass shooting involving the killing of 40-60 people to trigger public demand for changes to Gun laws. Yet, the number of gun related deaths in the USA since 1986 is greater than all the American deaths arising from every war and conflict that America has been involved with throughout its entire history. Even though this is a staggering statistic, it's only when a mass shooting of a relative handful of people gets beamed across the news channels of the world that we see strong and highly vocal demands for changes to gun laws. In the case of 9/11, it was the "reaction" to the attack that gave George Bush the justification for implementing his war on terror and everything that went along with it. He gave the world his now famous ultimatum "you're either with us or against us". Essentially, what he was saying was if you don't support us in the actions we are about to take you will be considered an enemy of America. And so it was, George Bush, with the support of his allies decided to plunge the world into one of the most ill thought out strategies for dealing with terrorism that we have ever witnessed.   He launched attacks on Afghanistan, he targeted Pakistan and he ultimately went for Iraq in a phoney war designed exclusively to implement regime change. Did he reduce the terror threat to the world? No - he simply made it worse. Meanwhile, ordinary citizens around the world have been subjected to a massive erosion of their basic freedoms. Take travel for example. We are all now subjected to the most rigorous security checks at airports around the world. Whilst these checks may have become a necessary evil in our lives, we have to ask ourselves how much of that checking is designed to make air travel safer and how much of it is to keep the terrorist fear-factor at the forefront of our minds. Certainly, the confiscation of liquids at airport security is just a joke that could be classified as little more than commercial exploitation of our fears. For sure, if security personnel at airports really believed that the liquids they confiscate could potentially be explosives, why would they simply toss them into a plastic garbage bin in a packed airport terminal? Then there is the now universal practice of exchanging passenger lists with different countries around the world. No longer can you travel overseas without someone at your destination checking you out before you arrive. The real irony of this is that while we have airport security throwing your plastic bottle of water into a trash can, all the home-gown, radicalised terrorists are free to roam the country committing their appalling acts of violence. The UK, the USA, France, Germany, Turkey, and Tunisia have all witnessed horrendous acts of terrorism, none of which have been committed by travellers from other countries entering through airport terminals. They've all been committed by home-grown terrorists who are largely disenfranchised members of their respective communities and who have been radicalised by people who live in countries where the war on terror has taken the most lives. As I said earlier, this is in no way an excuse for terrorism, but it does show the ludicrous situation we all face today. No-one in our political arena really cares about tackling the core problem. Instead, they just keep on implementing draconian measure to cause us all inconvenience while giving authorities the opportunity of monitoring our every move.

One of the main avenues for radicalisation has been the explosive growth in the Internet and, in particular, social networks. These allow direct communication between those that would do us harm and those who are susceptible to the message "you can make a difference". The problem we face is that disenfranchised people often feel useless and have no role to play in society. This is why they are easily targeted by the bad guys. For probably the first time in their lives they get the message that they are important and they can change the world by committing an act of terrorism. Unfortunately, governments have been powerless to stop these lines of communications. That's primarily due to all the do-good lefties who feel that we all have the right to remain anonymous on-line and can say fairly much anything we like without being held accountable. What absolute nonsense this is. It wouldn't be rocket science to implement regulations on social network operators to demand formal ID before allowing users to post obscene, threatening or other undesirable content over social network platforms. This would be no different to the rules for getting a telephone SIM card. In most countries, there is an obligation to prove who you are before you can get a telephone line, a broadband connection or a telephone SIM card. Surely, extending that requirement to social network operators to enable them to track down people who misuse the medium for terror or other socially unacceptable behaviour wouldn't be that difficult. For the privacy advocates, they should be told in very simple language if you have nothing to hide, you have nothing to fear. If you are going to act responsibly, your ID information will not be shared with government snoops. However, step over the line and you will be reported to the authorities. That would be tackling the problem at one of its principle base-camps. But, of course, this wouldn't suit most government agendas. They need to keep up the pressure by constantly keeping us focused on the problem. This way, we will continue to demand action and governments will find all sorts of new solutions that will involve each and every one of us in surrendering even more of our basic freedoms.

No doubt, if such a solution were ever to be implemented, I'm certain that the billionaire owners of social network sites will be the first to complain about the heavy additional cost of policing their networks. I wouldn't buy into that story either. If companies like Google can implement automated algorithms that trawl every communication that passes through their servers in order to target the world with billions of dollars of advertising, then I'm sure social network operators could do something similar to monitor their networks for anything that could be considered anti-social, hateful or terrorist related. Maybe a simple solution like this would keep us all a little safer whilst making people more responsible for what they do or say on-line. But, it isn't just the broadcast medium of the internet itself that has to be brought under some form of control. It's all those devices that terrorists could use against us that utilises this technology. Take for example drones. These relatively low cost devices are appearing everywhere. It seems that anyone with a few hundred bucks can simply go down to the local shopping mall and buy one of these things and use it in the most indiscriminate way possible without being subjected to any oversight by anyone. It's bad enough that some halfwit with a drone can send the device over your private back yard and film your wife or girlfriend lying naked on a sun-bed topping up her tan, or film your young children splashing around naked in your pool and then have the footage posted on line for everyone to see. But, what is really alarming is that some disenfranchised, home-grown terrorist can pack one of these devices with explosives or lethal chemicals and fly the thing into a sports arena, a shopping mall or just about any mass gathering of people. They could send it over a nuclear power station, or drop it onto a high-speed railway line. Already, we've seen the criminal fraternity using drones to smuggle drugs into prisons, we've witnessed drones flying dangerously close to commercial aircraft and we often see drones flying over large public gatherings. The continued, unfettered and unlicensed use of drone technology is a disaster just waiting to happen. But, of course, that's exactly what governments want to happen. It's going back to David Ike's description of how governments operate these days Problem, Reaction, Solution. At the moment, there is no problem so our politicians will do nothing to regulate the use of potentially dangerous technology that could be used by terrorists. Instead, they prefer to treat us like naughty children as a means of goading us into creating a problem so that we will eventually react and demand a solution to the problem. If you tell a child to stop doing something, they often challenge your authority by continually doing what you've asked them not to do until such point as the disobedience creates a problem for which you ultimately punish the child. At the moment, most governments are telling us how we should use drone technology but are not imposing any real obligations on us to follow their rules. We will, therefore, reach a point when someone uses the technology to create a really big problem (*probably a terrorist atrocity*). That will then give our politicians the ammunition they want to impose rules and regulations that will impede on our civil rights. The thing is, if rules and regulations are put in place before the problem occurs, those rules and regulations will only affect the few that use drone technology. However, by waiting for the problem, governments can impose more wider-reaching draconian measures over a broader spectrum of society.

I feel that many western democracies have overlooked one important fact about radicalised terrorists. They are the ultimate scholars. They learn fast and they react accordingly. The advent of the drone, and its devastating use by the military in places such as Pakistan, sends a very clear message to those who would radicalise sympathisers in the West. They no longer have to find totally unhinged radicals who don't mind blowing themselves up in a suicide vest. They can now target less unhinged people who would rather commit their acts of terrorism whist staying very much alive and undetected. Whilst US military drone strikes against terrorists are usually highly targeted, they often do cause death to innocent civilians. This is affectionately called "collateral damage" and is a term used to describe some form of inevitable consequence. That may well be the case, but the terrorists won't see it that way and neither will Western governments if a terrorist drone attack kills hundreds of innocent people in a Western democracy. The term "collateral damage" will never be used if that happens.

One of the major problems we face in tackling the scourge of terrorism is that we often don't know what these people want or what they are trying to achieve. It's not like a kidnapping where a ransom demand is made. Neither are today's terrorists like the IRA of yesterday where their acts of atrocities were accompanied by very clear political demands. Today, we're faced with violent extremists who make no demands and don't even tell us the reasons for their killing sprees. So, we are now left guessing. Clearly, a guessing game is not going to bring us any closer to finding a solution. Unfortunately, many of the world's politicians display a high degree of belligerence when it comes to "talking to the enemy". The strange thing is that western democracies can often engage with rebel factions in other countries to help them fight wars, but they seem incapable of engaging with those same people to find out what's bugging them. Until such time as they do engage in sensible discussion, we're never going to see the end of extremist violence, acts of terrorism or radicalisation within our own communities. This will be a major problem for future revolutionaries, in much the same way as it appears to be an insurmountable problem for today's politicians. The best we can hope for is that tomorrow's revolutionaries will garner a degree of sympathy from the radicals of the world. Maybe that will be the catalyst that enables us to start understanding the causes that drive factions to commit acts of terrorism. Maybe then we can start addressing the root cause of extremist violence instead of simply battling with the consequences of it.

The European Experiment

This section of the book takes us back to World War II because it was at the end of that war where the seeds of the European Union were sown. Essentially, after the war there was the inevitable share of the spoils among various countries involved in the conflict. France, in particular, had its eye firmly on Germany's steel and coal industries and the natural resources that fuelled them. As a result, France initially annexed the Saar Region of Germany and turned it into a French protectorate. They also had designs on the Ruhr area. Both of these regions formed the industrial heartland of Germany, so by gaining control of these two vital areas, Germany would be economically weakened to the advantage of the French. This caused much debate in Europe and the USA. But, after thrashing out a number of alternative plans, it was finally agreed to establish the European Coal and Steel Community (ECSC). The idea was simple enough; to regulate industrial production under a centralised authority. It was brought into effect by the Treaty of Paris in 1951 which was signed by France, Belgium. Italy, the Netherlands, Luxembourg and, what was then known as, West Germany. The establishment of the ECSC was the first step in a wider plan proposed by French Foreign Minister Robert Schuman in 1950 under which there would be much tighter integration of trade between the participating nations to eliminate competition between member states. This was the birth of what later became known as the Common Market. This was the mechanism that allowed other European countries to participate in the "Higher Authority" of the Common Market as a means of maintaining a peaceful existence among different European States. In the official declaration that created the ECSC, Schuman set out the ultimate aims of this new organisation. Clearly it would help ensure a peaceful and united Europe that would encourage world peace. It would also create a common market (*albeit in just coal and steel at the time*) across the European continent and it would help revitalise the shattered economies of Europe. However, Schuman did use some interesting phraseology. In particular, he made reference to a "Supranational Institution". This was discreetly edited by the French Economist Jean Monnet to read "Federation". He viewed the new organisation as being the first step in the creation of a federal Europe. Monnet also had other longer term plans. His vision was of a Europe that had a common central executive, a common currency, a centralised legal system, its own central bank and, most crucially, free movement of people, capital, goods and services across the borders of European countries. Of course, that was a vision expressed back in April 1952 and Monnet understood too well that this vision of a federal Europe wasn't going to be achieved overnight. He was reported as giving a speech in which he suggested that

European nations, with their long and diverse histories and their long standing cultures were not going to be easily persuaded to become part of a new federal Europe ruled by a centralised government. He was further reported as implying that in order to break down the nationalistic interests and sovereignty of European nations, it would be necessary to embark on a long-term plan spanning maybe 50 or 60 years to slowly but surely implement the changes so the citizens of Europe would never notice. Part of this plan was, as you would expect, the free movement of people across Europe. By doing this the demographic of each European country would change to the point that there would be little resistance to change when it came to the democratic process. Essentially, the more you can mix up the melting pot of people from different backgrounds and cultures, sovereignty and nationalistic barriers to a federal Europe would be removed. And that, my friends, is exactly what has happened. Even today, anyone visiting the European Parliament Visitor Centre will be greeted by a plaque that says:

"...national sovereignty is the root cause of the most crying evils of our time and of the steady march of humanity back to tragic disaster and barbarianism... The only final remedy for this supreme and catastrophic evil of our time is a federal union of the peoples..."

That quote is credited to Lord Lothian (*Philip Kerr*), a British politician, diplomat and newspaper editor who died in 1940. It's rather odd that a modern institution such as the EU chose to pick a quote such as this to adorn the walls of one of it's most cherished institutions. We can only assume that it typifies the thinking of today's European Union. It also reinforces the European belief that only a federal Europe with centralised control over its member States is the way forward. The writing is literally on the wall. However, this vision, although appearing everywhere in the EU history books, has never actually been sold to the people of Europe. They have all been conned by their national governments into believing that the EU is simply an economic club that allows for the harmonisation and free movement of goods, services, capital and people across member states.

Over a period of some 50-60 years we've seen the original ECSC transform into the Common Market. Later it became the European Economic Community and more recently it became the European Union. It extended its reach to just about every facet of both commercial and political life. It extended its influence over 28 countries. We've witnessed the introduction of the Council of Europe, The European Parliament, The European Courts, the introduction of the Euro and the establishment of a European Central Bank. We now have to contend with the European Commission, the European Court of Auditors, and the European

External Action Services. This is a massive bureaucratic machine that seeks to control the lives of every European citizen. It governs what we can buy, what we can consume and who we can do business with in the rest of the world. It can overturn national laws and force member states to implement any ridiculous piece of legislation it can dream up. For national politicians it's a dream come true. Now they don't have to justify the decisions they make. Instead they simply blame Europe for the unpopular and, often, ridiculous legislation they enact. You may be forgiven for thinking "why do national governments simply toe the line on this? Why are they not standing up to the EU and putting their own national population first?" Good questions and ones I'll answer in two words - Self-Interest. Politicians generally have a very short shelf-life. Once they reach their sell-buy date they're kicked out of office and have to go and do some of that stuff the rest of have to do to stay alive - WORK. But, the EU virtually guarantees national politicians a job for life. Because the EU does not democratically elect its executive, the EU can award life-long jobs to anyone who supports the great experiment. Therefore, as soon as national politicians get kicked out of office for failing to look after the interests of their national electorate, he or she gets a meal-ticket for life in one of the EU institutions. It's that simple.

The existence and expansion of the EU in recent years has already triggered a mild revolution across the continent. The punishment of Greece for failing to tackle its economic woes caused mass protests in the country. These were triggered through the imposition by the EU of draconian austerity measures on the Greek population as a condition of a financial bail-out. The EU demanded significant changes to the way people earned their money, the basis upon which they could retire and the amount of pensions they could receive. Yet, despite a resounding rejection of these measures by the Greek public in a 2015 referendum, the Greek government decided to ignore the wishes of the people and accept the conditions anyway. Germany also had a mild revolution due to the German Government's open door policy towards migrants fleeing from countries like Syria. That problem was felt across Europe as individual countries struggled to contain the swarming masses eager to get to Germany. But, the real slap in the face for Europe was the UK decision to exit the EU club altogether in 2016. By a slim majority, UK citizens had suddenly woken up to the perceived madness of the EU and it's policies. They voted in a national referendum to leave the EU. This was a very dangerous moment for EU institutions. The concern wasn't so much about the UK leaving the club, but was more about possible contagion to other EU member states. This has created a state of alert across Europe. Whilst countries such as France and the Netherlands and, more recently, Germany have successfully stemmed the flow of support for right-wing national political parties, it's all too apparent that if the UK's departure from the EU proves to be a resounding success, other European countries will think again about whether they should remain a member of this undemocratic machine called the EU. So, the table has been set. The EU MUST ensure that the UK's decision to Brexit from Europe will be a total disaster. They must be seen to be punishing the UK for its belligerent attitude towards the great EU experiment. If they fail to dish-out adequate punishment, it may well signal the end of the EU as we know it today.

The problem the UK faces in its exit negotiations is that it lost the ability to exert its power. The UK, in 2017, had a weak government with an even more pathetic opposition. It also comprised a smattering of other political ideologies that focused on narrow self interests who would use Brexit as leveraging to gain political advantages for their narrow causes. The country was facing a possible monumental crisis under which you would expect politicians to come together for the sake of the British people. But, you can't expect such a magnanimous response from today's career politicians. All they care about is themselves, so they will cause as much disruption as possible just to look after their own interests.   It's against this fragmented backdrop of UK politics that the EU emboldened itself and embarked on what appears to be gang warfare against the UK. The first thing on their precious EU agenda was the divorce settlement with figures of €100 billion being bandied around. They seem to have forgotten that since joining in 1973, the UK has already invested over half a trillion Euros into the EU and its massive bureaucratic machine. The EU also started the divorce proceedings with some really unhelpful comments such as "the UK cannot cherry-pick what it wants from Europe". It wanted to deny the UK access to any of the benefits previously enjoyed as an EU member state unless the UK agreed to implement the four basic freedoms laid down by the EU. These are free movement of goods, capital, services and labour. Clearly, if the UK agreed to this it would be like staying in the EU but without having a voice at the table. The Brexiteers in the UK would have something to say if that was agreed to. But, strangely, there are UK politicians who actually wanted to ignore the will of the people and have the UK agree to this demand, it was termed "a soft Brexit". For the UK's part, the response has been abysmal. What the UK should have done was to simply address the EU and deliver a well thought through historic lecture along with the country's letter of resignation. The lecture should have been on the lines of:

"During World War II, every continental member state was either under direct German occupation, under German administration or were sitting on the fence leaving their neighbours to fend for themselves (notably Spain, Portugal, Ireland and Sweden). Some countries became allies of Nazi Germany (most notably Italy) whilst other countries established

governments in exile, leaving their citizens to organise themselves into resistance groups that could fight alongside the allied forces. The UK, for its part, was never a target of Nazi Germany and had little or no reason to get involved in the war. However, the UK was drawn into the conflict because of a promise it made to Poland in 1939 under which the UK (with the tacit support of the French) guaranteed Polish independence. When Germany invaded Poland the UK honoured that pledge and declared war on Germany. In fact, the only two countries that made a conscious decision to free Europe from the Tyranny of Adolf Hitler were the UK and the Soviet Union. So, the UK and the Soviet Union are the countries that gave Europe the democratic freedoms it enjoys today. Instead of showing gratitude to these two countries for liberating continental Europe, The EU has decided that one of those countries, the UK, should be punished for wishing to leave the European club. Shame on you Europe - you have very short memories."

Whilst such a lecture would not have gone down too well in the hallowed halls of the Brussels bureaucratic machine, it would have made then British Prime Minister, Theresa May, a national hero back home. A lost opportunity if I ever saw one. As for that letter of resignation, it should have gone something like this:

Dear Sirs,

The UK hereby formally tenders its resignation from the European Union with immediate effect. In so doing, we will not be paying any divorce bills that you may conjure up. On the contrary, we view our half a trillion Euros contribution to the EU thus far as an investment for which we expect to receive some form of dividends in the future, either in cash, goods, services or concessions on future trading relations. In removing ourselves from the EU, we will preserve the rights of EU citizens currently working, living or being educated in the UK and we expect you to afford the same courtesy to UK citizens living in other EU member states.

We have no intention of imposing any tariffs on goods or services imported into the UK from EU member states. To do so would be little more than a consumption tax on UK consumers - something we are not prepared to impose on our citizens. However, if you wish to impose such taxes on EU consumers for British goods - go and sell the idea to your respective electorates.

EU citizens will continue to be welcomed to British shores subject to our immigration policies. Tourists will be offered free visas on demand at ports of entry, whilst those wishing to come to the UK for work or education will be free to make application for extended stays of more than 3 months.

It should also be noted that we will not be wasting our tax-payer's money or diplomatic resources negotiating the terms of our exit from the EU. Quite simply, there is nothing to negotiate so why should we waste two years of our time for nothing. If you wish to spend the next two years discussing the matter between yourselves and deciding on an appropriate punishment for the UK, by all means do - I'm sure you will have many EU tax-payer funded dinners and fine wines to help you through the arduous process.

Finally, should you find yourself in a position where your security is again threatened by an unfriendly invader, please feel free to call on us for any assistance you may need in repelling the scoundrels. We may require a security deposit before involving ourselves in any future skirmishes because we don't want to be left with a bill from the Americans that could take 60 years to repay, like the last war.

Yours

The UK government

Unfortunately, our bumbling politicians and their political correctness has meant the UK didn't adopt such a plain-speaking line. Instead, they fell into the EU trap of being forced into polite negotiations in which the EU do all the demanding while the UK sits in the naughty corner taking its punishment without so much as a whimper.

The fact remains that the EU has become a little too much for many people to bear. It's so disorganised that it has to have two parliaments in two different countries in order to pacify the original members (*neither of which were nations that ultimately bestowed peace and freedom on continental Europe*). That little exercise of moving the parliament between two centres like a traveling circus costs the EU taxpayers circa €130 million a year. The whole EU bureaucratic machine is a juggernaut just waiting to crash. The whole institution must either be scrapped or reformed from the ground up.   It really is quite sickening to see hoards of European leaders and ministers pouring into numerous EU summits in their private jets and fleets of black limousines complete with an army of police outriders to make sure no harm comes to them. The strange thing is, many of these politicians are virtually unknown outside of their own countries. As for the EU commissioners and their President, none of them are democratically elected by the European public. That's a job left to MEP's. Most Commissioners come from the ranks of failed politicians who are proposed to the

European Parliament. The only real elected body is the European Parliament which is composed of MEP's elected by the citizens of each member state. However, such is the level of disinterest in Europe, less than 40% of the EU population of eligible voters actually bother to cast a ballot for candidate MEP's. The problem with this fine body of people is that they cannot propose or make laws. All they can do is say yes or no to legislation proposed by the EU commission. If they vote overwhelmingly no, the legislation is often brought back to the table until they eventually say yes. And, where does that legislation come from? Well, it certainly doesn't get proposed by the ordinary citizens. In fact, much EU legislation is brought about through lobby groups. If you thought the USA was the only country in the world who's legislation was driven by lobby groups, think again. Europe is number two in the world.

Those lobby groups are representatives of some of the world's largest, European-based corporations. The most notorious of the lobbyists is the European Round Table. This little organisation (*affectionately calling itself an Advocacy Group*) comprises a membership of over 50 European industrial leaders who's sole purpose is to give an unfair advantage to European business through the promotion of legislative barriers to market entry from outside of the EU. As such, they not only propose policy to the EU, but they actively create policy documents and reports that the European Commission simply sign off as their own policies which are ultimately put in front of parliament for final approval. That's how lazy European Commissioners are. They can't be bothered to look at issues that may be affecting ordinary citizens, so they get organisations like the ERT to come up with ideas for new legislation that only favours the major corporations. What is really irritating is that the ERT has almost exclusive rights in accessing the Commissioners. Whenever the ERT calls one of its secret meetings, the Commissioners are there with their top people to make sure that every demand and wish of this powerful lobby group is heard.

For the rest of the EU citizenship, they have to accept notional pacifiers - regulations that appear on the surface to be doing something good for the ordinary folk but, in reality, are nothing more than little throw-away incentives to keep us right behind the European experiment. Take, for example, the EU's open skies policy. This enables EU airlines to operate freely across Europe whilst keeping non-EU competitors locked out. What has this done for consumers? Well, it's allowed a whole raft of European budget airlines to emerge who regularly fleece the traveling public by offering a third-rate service that is little more than a cattle-truck thinly disguised as air travel. The notion that they have given us low-cost travel across Europe is simply another one of those EU negotiated deals with airline operators that allows commercial interests to capitalise on the naivety of the traveling public. The EU has allowed these bucket-shop airlines to advertise very cheap tickets to the more popular cities and tourist destinations of Europe. So, whilst we have all been enticed by an advertised bargain price deal of an airline ticket from the UK to sunny southern Spain at say €20, the reality is somewhat different. Firstly, you have to find that deal. If you're lucky enough to be one of those who caught the small number of seats available at this price, the booking process often reveals that you simply can't get a ticket at this price. By the time you've added in a checked piece of baggage, and possibly a piece of hand baggage, you've already doubled the advertised price. But, it doesn't stop there. If you want to be assured of a seat next to your travelling companion or family member, there is another charge to pay in the form of a seat allocation charge. Then there is the booking fee. I never understood why these airlines charge a booking fee when it's the customer that does all the work! When you get to the end of the process, you'll be suddenly hit with taxes or fuel surcharges which can easily double the price you're at at this stage. Oh, and don't forget, the only way you can pay for this ticket is with a credit or debit card. Guess what, they charge you extra for this privilege also. Now, if you forget to check-in online, you'll be hit by another big charge at the airport for checking in at a desk. If, during your flight, you decide you would like a snack or a drink, you'll be hit with a charge that would be commensurate with a top restaurant, even though you are only buying a cheese sandwich and can of cola. This is what the EU has done for us. Kidology has come into play yet again. The EU public actually believe they're getting a bargain price but, the reality is that they could often get a cheaper deal by purchasing a regular, all-inclusive, scheduled airline ticket from a national carrier.

The same has happened with the telecommunications industry in Europe. In 2017, the EU trumpeted the good news that mobile data and voice call roaming charges were to come to an end in Europe. This meant that anyone traveling to another EU country would be able to use their mobile devices at the same call or data prices that they would pay if they were in their home country. Of course, anyone reading the small print would soon discover this wasn't an abolition of roaming charges at all. It was, in fact, a "phased relaxation" of charges for those who may be on vacation for a relatively short period of time. If you are one of the many EU citizens who may be contracted to work in another EU state for say three or four months, you would soon discover that your phone operator would cancel this arrangement after a few weeks and start charging you higher tariffs. The real blow to consumers are those who have pre-paid plans that give them a fixed number of minutes of national or international calls plus a specific volume of data transfer for a fixed period of time for a fixed rate. Anyone on this type of plan will suddenly find themselves unable to utilise the service they've already paid for. Instead, they will be faced with having to top up their SIM credit so that they can pay for usage at a higher rate than they would back home. This was just another deal done between the EU and mobile telephone operators to ensure that no competition could exist between European phone companies. Is this important? yes it is, because there are supposed to be no barriers to the free movement of goods and services between EU member states. But, this isn't the case with phone companies. Whilst a telecoms provider in say Romania can offer a fixed price package involving 200 minutes of national calls, 100 minutes of international calls and 20GB of data transfer over a 30 day period for €8.00 , this package is denied to someone living in say Spain where the same operator charges €12.00 for a package that offers a mere 30 minutes of local calls only and 2GB of data transfer over the same period. Such is the lunacy of EU regulations and the absolute fallacy of the four freedoms that are supposed to be enshrined into EU laws.

The notion that the EU has no commercial borders is, in itself, a total whitewash of the the reality. Whilst there are no tariffs charged when moving goods or services from one EU member State to another, the EU does allow individual States to impose their own rules and regulations when it comes to excise duties. For example, I can buy a half decent bottle of wine in France, Italy or Spain for about €2.00 but that same bottle of wine can cost between £5 and £10 in the UK.

This is because the UK government is free to add on any excise duties it feels appropriate. The same is true of tobacco products. Whilst we shouldn't encourage the use of tobacco, the fact is, while tobacco products remain legal to buy there shouldn't be a massive price difference between EU member states. A pack of cigarettes in Romania or Bulgaria would cost about €3-€4 whereas, in the UK and Ireland it would cost between €10-€15.

It would appear that our next revolutionaries will have their work cut out when it comes to the European Union. It won't be a simple question of whether countries remain or leave the EU. After all, that is a decision that should be decided democratically by the people. However, such important decisions should be based on truth rather than deception, so the job of our revolutionaries will be to ensure that truth prevails so we can all make sound decisions. As a trade organisation, there is little intrinsically wrong with the EU and its stated objectives. The problem is, few of us actually know what the true objectives are. If we did know, we could choose to maintain the EU for a wide range of positive reasons and reform those areas where EU policies, and ambitions may not be in our best interests. Sadly, many citizens of the EU base their views and opinions on political spin rather than concerted research that will highlight the realities. It's easier for us to listen to those for or against the EU who may cite very narrow, self-interest agendas as a means of persuading us of the merits or otherwise of maintaining this large economic bloc to the point where it becomes a dictatorial political mess. Certainly, the political side of the monster needs to be tamed. Sovereignty is not something that nations can give up very easily, particularly among European nations that have very long histories and cultural/political backgrounds. Its become common place in Europe to label anyone who is anti-EU as racist, stupid, ignorant nationalists. These words come out of the mouths of politicians as well as EU supporters. They effectively divide nations into them and us, just like George W. Bush when he uttered his only unambiguous comment that we could all understand " You're either with us or against us". In fact, we haven't come very far from the days of Adolf Hitler. He convinced a large proportion of the population of Germany that those who were against his madman ideology were enemies of the state that have to be rounded up, interrogated, tortured and ultimately sent to death camps strategically placed around Europe. We are now seeing it all over again through the imposition of punishments for EU member states who's populations may decide to go against EU policies.

It should also be remembered that nationalism is still quite an important factor in the human condition. Nationalism is something that drives empathy and ultimately creates trust. If you are an English person, you could wander the streets of the UK every day for a year and never meet someone you know. As a consequence, you wouldn't easily find empathy with the people you bump into. Now put yourself in a position where you may find yourself sitting in a bar in Moscow. If you hear someone speaking English, you're more likely to strike up a conversation with them knowing they come from the UK. National empathy comes into play. You may even exchange contact information. Your new-found friend may even suggest you try out their favourite restaurant in Moscow. They may tell you about the great food, excellent service and reasonable prices. Now here's the strange thing - you're very likely to trust that recommendation. You will thank them and assure them that you will give it a try. That's a lot different from you bumping into a complete stranger in the UK who may tell you to try out a particular restaurant - you'd think they were crazy. Now put yourself again in that Moscow bar. If you suddenly hear an Italian, a German or a Dutch accent, you're highly unlikely to strike up a conversation on the basis that you are from the same continent. Consequently, there will be no empathy and, ultimately, no trust. This is something that the EU has totally overlooked in their quest to create a federal Europe. National identity and, thus empathy and trust simply will not exist. We've already seen it in action during the Brexit negotiations. There is absolutely no trust between all sides of the negotiating table. There is no trust because there is no empathy that binds the parties together. This is why I suggested earlier in this chapter that the UK should have made a point about the UK's role in giving Europe its democratic freedoms after World War II. By doing so, it would have served as a gentle reminder that the UK and the rest of Europe once enjoyed a great deal of empathy and trust. We were bound together to resolve a major problem and we succeeded. This simple reminder could have easily resonated with the rest of Europe and helped ease the tensions at the negotiating table.

It may be quite a long struggle to democratise the EU to the point where ordinary citizens are again in control of their political masters and can freely voice their opinions and concerns without fear of being negatively labeled racist or nationalist, but it is something that must happen if we are to avoid total dictatorship by an unelected body. Our politicians must learn the lesson that dividing nations in such an obscene and hateful manner can do no good. They must also understand that throwing 27 or 28 nations into a single melting pot will ultimately be the biggest fail of all time. They will simply break down national empathy and trust and put in it's place a rather bland group of people that have very little in common except, maybe, business or financial interests. There will, of course, be those EU supporters who will cite the USA as a perfect example of a federal state that has thrived on the melting pot principal. What such people fail to understand is that the USA was founded by Europeans voluntarily going to

America to build a brand new country. They had that common goal and therefore developed that all important empathy. They now all consider themselves American - one nation, regardless of which state they live in. Europe will never reach that same level. It may be a good trading bloc, but it will never be considered, no matter how hard the European bureaucrats try and dictate, a true country. It will always be a group of individual nations and blending them together through free movement is never going to change that.

The Competitive Environment

Let's start this chapter with a look at the definition of "Competition".

...the activity or condition of striving to gain or win something by defeating or establishing superiority over others.

It's an interesting definition because although governments will always tell us mere mortals that competition in the commercial world is a good thing, the reality is that, by definition, it involves winners and losers. Some people will be able to exercise their superiority over others by obtaining goods and services at an advantageous price, whilst the less superior beings amongst us will end up paying more to subsidise those who would gain financial advantages at the expense of the majority. So, whilst we have politicians telling us that healthy competition in the commercial arena is the key to lowering consumer prices, if we take a closer look at the facts it will be seen that this isn't always the case. In previous chapters we've discussed the rich/poor divide and we've touched upon the rise of technology in the promotion of consumer goods and services. We've also touched upon how the financial system has been engineered to disadvantage the majority of people in favour of promoting ever spiralling economic growth. In the commercial world of consumer sales and marketing, all these areas of discontent come together in spectacular fashion to ensure that we not only keep on buying stuff we don't really need, but also that we pay far more for some goods and services than we have to.

As highlighted in the previous chapter, one of the most annoying of these "rip-offs" is budget airlines. They, and our respective governments, will go to great lengths to convince us that low cost airlines have empowered us all to travel the world at very low cost. As we've already discussed, those bargain prices often promoted by budget airlines, in many cases, have significant extra charges hidden behind the facade of the advertising. But, despite these seemingly low prices, the actual profit margins of budget airlines aren't that much different from traditional national carriers. Therefore, some passengers must be helping keep profit margins within reasonable levels. Of course, apart from the misleading "advertised price" deception, there are other tricks deployed by low-cost airlines to ensure that we stay hooked onto their kidology. How many times have you tried to book a flight and been presented with a whole range of prices from which to choose? If you look closely at some of the lower prices, you will see those magic words "only X seats available at this price". What they don't tell you is how many ACTUAL seats are still available on the flight. You see, airlines will only allocate a certain number of seats at lower prices in an attempt to kid us all into believing that they are offering a great deal. If the truth be known, probably less than 20% of aircraft capacity will be offered at a low price, with everyone else paying progressively higher prices the closer the booking gets to departure date. The end result is that out of 120 passengers there may be as many as 40+ different fares being charged even though everyone is crammed into the same tiny seats, leaving from the same departure airport, arriving at the same destination and all will be offered the same high-priced food and beverage on board along with all that other stuff that airlines try to sell you. Now it has to be mentioned that it's not only the budget airlines that use this pricing strategy. Almost all national flag carriers have started adopting the same system. Essentially, once a particular flight is opened for reservation (*around three months prior to departure*) there will be special low price offers to those who can book early. This is essentially a "bums on seats" strategy designed to cover the basic costs of getting the flight in the air and to its ultimate destination. Once there are sufficient "bums on seats" to achieve this, the prices start to get progressively higher. If you are one of those unfortunates who book at the 11th hour (*such as business travellers*) you're most likely to be hit with the most expensive fares. If there are insufficient passengers to make the flight economical, the airlines can simply pull the plug on the flight and move everyone onto an alternative flight. This strategy may well have existed prior to budget airlines, however, modern technology has made it really simple for airlines to automate the process of setting seat prices. Complex algorithms are used in online booking systems which automatically adjust prices in accordance with booking demand. And, what about those online booking systems? They present a situation where you, the consumer, must do everything that the airlines and their travel agency partners used to do for us. We have to select our flight, complete the passenger details, go through the long list of extras, allocate our own seats, check in both hold and hand baggage and print out our own tickets and boarding cards. The airlines have no booking costs whatsoever and yet they still charge you a booking fee. If, like many human beings, you make an error or typo along the way, correcting the problem can cost you dearly. Trying to phone an airline customer service department to correct an error (*even one as simple as a typo on a passenger name*) will normally involve you calling a premium rate number where your call will be answered automatically and then leave you on hold to generate more income for the airline. When you do eventually get to speak to someone, you will inevitably be told that there will be a significant charge to change anything on your reservation.   As for cancellations or changing travel dates, you can, in most instances, say goodbye to the fee you paid for your original flight. Furthermore, the new flight you're offered will not be at one of those bargain prices you saw advertised on the airline's web site.

If you think that airlines treat their premium passengers any differently, think again. When I booked a business class ticket from Barcelona to Seoul, I was offered a fare by a well known national flag carrier of €2,308. This was a restricted ticket that didn't provide for a refund, but could be changed upon payment of an additional fee of circa €200 plus the difference in airfare. The airline also offered a fully flexible business ticket at a price of €4,525 which would allow me to change or cancel the reservation without penalty. Now, you may think this is a fair approach to flight pricing, and I would agree. However, there is a snag. Only a certain number of SEATS are allocated to passengers who want the cheaper of the two options, even though passengers on either tariff are travelling in the same cabin with the same facilities. So, although there maybe 20 seats in the business cabin, only a small number are available for use by restricted ticket passengers. The rest of the seats could be completely unoccupied but the airline simply won't sell those seats to passengers who want a restricted ticket - how mad is that! I've seen the same scenario with economy tickets on national airlines. Very often you see fully flexible and semi flexible tickets for sale. The difference in price is quite substantial so clearly, passengers who have no intention of changing their travel dates are unlikely to pay the full price. However, the airlines will restrict the numbers to ensure that only a small number of passengers can take advantage of the lower fares. Basically, it seems the airlines would rather have an aircraft full of passengers that could all demand a refund, rather than an aircraft full of passengers who wouldn't have that option. It doesn't make sense until you realise that very few passengers will actually cancel or change their reservation - something the airlines know too well and have built into their seat pricing algorithms!

It's not only airlines that have found all sorts of ways to maximise their profits at the consumer's expense. Almost all public transport systems have started using the same strategies. In the UK, for example, the train services have a bewildering range of prices for tickets. Some are priced according to the time and date of travel with the most expensive tickets being those sold to people who are forced to use the train service to get to and from work every day. These trains are often packed to the seams with high-paying passengers, whilst those that can organise their travel between the peak hours can often travel in spacious comfort at a much lower price. The national bus network in the UK also has some strange pricing anomalies. Most intercity bus services are run on routes that often stop-off at major cities along the route. So, someone booking a journey from say Manchester to London, is likely to travel a route that takes them via Birmingham where new passengers can be picked up and some passengers dropped off. A ticket from Manchester to London can be quite expensive, particularly at peak times. However, if you book two tickets, one from Manchester to Birmingham and one from Birmingham to London, you often find that you've made a significant cost saving and yet you won't necessarily leave the bus you're traveling on - go figure!

There are, of course, more serious issues raised by commercial competitiveness. Nowhere is this more prevalent than in energy pricing. Again, taking the UK as an example, consumers are faced with a bewildering choice of tariffs but there are just six main energy suppliers. The idea is to create absolute confusion among consumers so that those with the least amount of knowledge on the subject of energy supply and consumption will pay far more than those who have the ability to continually monitor energy prices and consumption and switch to cheaper suppliers when circumstances dictate. In an attempt to display openness and fairness, the big six suppliers all contribute to price comparison websites where consumers can make an assessment of their energy consumption and patterns and select the best possible tariff from the huge choice out there. The problem is, people don't always understand what they have to to do and, in many cases, simply don't have the time to regularly monitor their consumption and make price comparisons. And why should they? Energy is a resource governed by a number of cost variables, but those variables apply to every supplier (*such as the price of oil*). Therefore, all energy should be piped into the homes of consumers at a fixed and known rate. There may be variances such as day and night tariffs, but that should be it. Why should two families living in identical homes on the same street with much the same energy consumption be paying different rates for their energy? The answer, as you would expect, is "profiteering". Instead of governments creating a competitive environment, they've simply allowed the formation of cartels who can set their prices to maximise profits, usually at the expense of the most vulnerable members of society. People such as pensioners or those surviving on benefits or low incomes are often penalised by the energy companies. These are the people who often have to resort to pre-paid energy meters in their homes. Price comparison websites are no use to these people. The price they have to pay for their energy consumption is top dollar and they have little choice but to pay up when the lights go off.

Other areas of commercial competitiveness centre around the telecommunications industry. Not only are there wide variations in the tariffs that consumers pay, but there are also very significant variances in the levels of service provided in different parts of a country. In Spain, for example, if you live near a coastal highway or in the centre of a major city, the chances are that your telecoms provider will supply you with a fast, fibre-optic broadband connection. If, however, you live in the suburbs or inland, you will be lucky to get a service anywhere near the same level. Despite these anomalies, most telecoms providers will charge the same tariffs no matter how good or bad your broadband connection. In mobile telephony, there are a huge number of different tariffs that consumers can choose from. Each will come with their compliment of free calls, SMS messages and Data transfer etc. The prices charged will vary considerably between suppliers and different plans. This, again, is simple profiteering. For example, if a consumer chooses a plan that costs €20 per month and it includes 3 GB of data transfer, 100 minutes of local calls and maybe 20 minutes of International calls, that may seem like a good deal IF YOU USE IT ALL UP. In some countries, the telecoms companies were quick to notice that some of these plans were simply not being fully utilised in the time frames set for consumption (*normally 30 days*), so in order to grab a larger slice of market share, they introduced lower cost packages that offered ridiculous levels of consumption such as 20 GB data transfer, 1,000 minutes of local calls, and 400 minutes of international calls. In the vast majority of cases, consumers who buy these plans only use a fraction of the consumption available to them. However, the telecoms companies continue to attract new customers against the promise of perceived low price plans that offer ridiculous levels of consumption that the vast majority of people simply can't utilise.

Furthermore, all these customers keep on paying the fixed amount every month without even checking to see how much of the package is being consumed. Meanwhile, those who simply purchase a SIM card and choose to pay whatever the standard call, SMS or data transfer rate is, will pay far more per call or MB of consumption, but may actually be paying less each month to their service provider due to their low level of consumption. Likewise, those who pay for a fixed price plan that includes a free handset may also end up paying more than they have to. A good smartphone can be purchased outright (*sim-free*) for about €150 in Europe. However, that same handset could be offered as part of a €29 per month package deal that includes some element of consumption. The downside is that the contract may be for 24 months and you may use up the included consumption quite quickly and end up with some heavy bills at the end of each month. So, the minimum you will be paying under contract will be €696 over the contract term for a €150 smartphone and a basic level of consumption. This, of course, is only possible because of the intervention of finance companies and smartphone manufacturers who want to get their products into a prominent market position. For sure, the cost of the smartphone (*even the top-end ones*) to the telecoms companies will be about half of the retail price. Furthermore, these phones will be locked to the services of the telecoms provider for the duration of the contract. So, with a little help from the world of finance and smartphone manufacturers, telecoms companies can lock you into lucrative contracts that will continue to fuel their thirst for profits for years at a time.

Of course, telecoms providers have now created services that other dominant companies can capitalise on. I remember a time not so long ago when I could buy a Sky Satellite TV package that would include a dish, a set-top box and installation for about £30 per month. This would enable me to watch about 500 channels of mindless TV 24/7. Nowadays, companies such as Sky, Virgin Media, Amazon and BT in the UK can offer all sorts of packages that include, premium sports channels, movies on demand, multi-room, multi channel, catch up TV and the ability to record endless hours of that mind numbing TV that gets piped in from around the globe. Not only do these new services cost considerably more than the old Sky Satellite system, they also need you to have a fibre broadband subscription. Whilst we may think this is great progress, it's all kidology again. There is no way that anyone in their remaining lifetime can watch all that TV - there just aren't enough hours left in our lives to watch it all. So, again we see consumers paying for stuff that they simply cannot consume. In those households with young teenagers (*and some older ones*) who you would expect to sit in front of a TV watching all this stuff, the chances are that they are too busy playing those expensive video games. So, much of the TV and movie stuff is simply not getting consumed. Meanwhile, the TV manufacturers are having a field-day. The advent of multichannel, multi room systems has seen an explosion in TV sales. Whereas at one time the average household would have a single TV, households today are more likely to have a big, flat screen TV in every room of the house. The social impact of this phenomena is likely to come back and bite us all in the butt at some future date. Families no longer sit together or engage in common conversation. Family members, including children, can simply wander off into their own space within the home and tune into anything that takes their interest. And then the parents display shock and horror when they realise that their little boy or girl has been engaged in some unsavoury antics in the world of the Internet, or has been tuned into unsuitable program content on their shiny new IP TV package. As for the new breed of commercial broadcasters, they have completely destroyed the simple pleasure of being a spectator at a sporting event. In the UK, it was almost a preserve of the working man to go see his local football team play every Saturday afternoon. Football matches were a competitive rivalry between towns and cities. In today's world, thanks in large part to the huge amounts of money paid to football leagues for broadcasting rights, the cost of tickets to matches has gone through the roof, and the chances of you finding players that actually hail from the town or city who's name is associated with the club is very slim indeed.

Football clubs now get hundreds of millions in revenues which they use to buy players from all over the world. They also get commercial sponsorship which allows the club to produce replicas of the team's strip that they then sell to football fans the world over at astronomical prices. What those ardent fans have largely failed to realise is that they are paying a small fortune for clothing that sports the name of the club's sponsor, effectively paying for the privilege of becoming a walking billboard for yet another major corporation.

This whole world of commercialism and the competition that exists between the major players in the consumer markets has been no accident. Its been a deliberate act by governments to create a consumer society that can keep that "money-go-round" spinning in ever faster circles. Governments cannot let the spending spree come to an end. If they did, there would be another major financial disaster worse than the one we experienced in 2007/2008. So, by creating a so-called competitive environment, consumers are actively encouraged to go from company to company looking for, what appears on the surface to be, great consumer deals. At every step, consumers end up parting company with more and more of their hard-earned cash. As people swap from one energy supplier within the cartel to another, they invariably incur costs and charges. As they buy something as mundane as an IP entertainment package, they boost the fortunes of telecoms companies and TV manufacturers. They also boost the fortunes of those IP broadcasters who not only get a big subscription from consumers, they also generate huge advertising revenues from major corporations who promote even more consumer goods and services to the sheep-like subscribers. Think about it, we're actually paying TV broadcasters to show us advertising! That is sheer lunacy.

Competition is also going to cause us major problems at street level. As more and more people actually succumb to this nonsense, there is an overwhelming fear that if we don't all join in we'll be left as social outcasts. For those that can't maintain an income sufficient to fuel the debts needed to maintain this endless cycle of spending, they will eventually become resentful of those who can simply keep their consumerism at the centre of their lives. Such resentment will lead to problems as the gap between the perceived rich and the poor widens. Our next revolutionaries will, most likely, stem from the ranks of those who simply can't keep up with the financial demands on consumers. These will also, most likely, be the people who have experienced the rough-end of the competitive stick. The ones who have paid through the nose so that those seemingly smarter members of society could capitalise on the best commercial deals. People will start to resent the fact that their inability to respond positively to consumer competition has forced them into subsidising others who will be perceived as more well-off or more clever. This isn't a good base camp to set off from if you want the world to come together for future change. Therefore, there will be an inevitable period through which the "them and us" traits of the human condition will rear its ugly head. That's when the revolution will start to happen. Hopefully, it won't materialise in the usual way of pitch battles between the factions, or the looting of homes, but it is likely to be messy.

The consumer madness that we are witnessing today isn't just confined to major commercial players who have created the perception of competition as a means of increasing profits. It's also a problem that stems from companies making and selling branded products. Whilst there is some merit in protecting brands from highjacking, there has to be some modicum of sympathy for those who do err on the wrong side of the law by making fake copies of high-priced consumer brands. To understand this just look at what "Brand Value" is all about. It's essentially a value that is added to a product to cover the cost of intense, and often expensive marketing. In other words, if the marketing costs were kept to a minimum, there would be little reason to add a brand value to anything (*other than the fact that it may have a design patent which may have cost a lot of money to register*). Let's put this into some sort of perspective. If we look at most expensive consumer brands, particularly in clothing, what we find is that the brand company has had the products manufactured in the sweat-shops of Asia at rock bottom prices. They then bring the product back to Western democracies and embark on very expensive marketing campaigns to get the target market (*mainly wealthy people*) to buy the product at very high prices. Meanwhile, a low-life bootlegger comes along and decides to go back to the sweat-shops of Asia to have a near identical version of the product manufactured so that it can be sold to the less wealthy members of society who aspire to own the product, but simply can't afford it. Now we have to ask two questions. Is the consumer who buys the low-price knock-off ever likely to become a customer for the real thing? Question number two, is the consumer who CAN afford to buy the real thing, likely to be persuaded to buy a cheap knock-off? In both cases it can be safely assumed the answer will be no. So, if there is little or no monetary loss to the brand owner, why do they go out of their way to round up the fakers and their products? If I was a cynical person I would perhaps wonder why the brand owner shouldn't be happy to pay the fakers to keep going in order to keep their brands in the public eye. Of course, the argument would be that they don't wish to have their brand associated with or cheapened by an inferior product. But, whilst this may be a perfectly valid argument in the area of fashion or perfumes, the same isn't true of food brands.

A food brand is often just a name or a trademark that is owned by someone who doesn't actually manufacture anything. Instead, they go to large specialist food processing companies and have them package an existing product. Only the packaging is changed to reflect the brand and for that consumers are forced to pay a premium price for the product. Many supermarket own brands are produced by the same factories that package products for big brand names and yet they are considerably cheaper than the branded counterpart. So here we see that brand value has nothing to do with quality, but has everything to do with applying an additional margin of profit to a standard product that does little more than line the pocket of the brand owner. And who pays? The consumer of course. Well-known brands in the food industry are also becoming notorious for fooling us into increasing their profit margins through packaging deception. Most notable were the confectionery brands that decided to reduce the weight of their actual product whilst maintaining the physical dimensions of the packaging (*confectionery brands were a prime example*). Cereal breakfast food manufactures are also pulling the same trick. In the EU, for example, there are specific standard weights for cereal foods ranging from 125 gms all the way up to 1.5kg. As an average shopper, you may see two packs of cereals on the shelf in identically sized cartons. However, on close inspection of the weights, you may notice one has 500 gms of content whilst the other only has 375 gms. At first glance, the 375 gms pack may look better value, but not necessarily if you start looking at the cost per gram. This packaging deception is used frequently by food brands to disguise price increases. They simply keep the old pack size but reduce the quantity of product. Very often, a breakfast cereal box is only half full anyway (*supposedly to protect the content from damage!*). Certain products are more difficult to disguise. A good example is preserves such as jam. In the UK a 1 lb jar of jam or honey was the norm. However, progressively the jars have become smaller to the point where the current average weight is 375 gms, or in some cases, 200 gms. Whilst this isn't actually package deception, it is a form of deception because the price per unit (*jar*) may stay the same, but it's physical size gets smaller over time. The gradual decrease in size often isn't noticeable as new sizes are slowly introduced.

Branding is one of those strange anomalies that allow companies to maintain high profit margins and market domination even where competition is rife. They do it through clever advertising that convinces us that we must be associated with the brand in order to show others that we are "brand savvy". The advertising also instills a degree of trust. The brand may be over 100 years old and therefore we instinctively trust the product more than we may trust a new kid on the block. Of course, that's absolute nonsense. All food sold on supermarket shelves must meet high standards of quality and hygiene by law. So a 100 year old brand isn't going to be any better quality than a brand that was launched last week. There may be some perceptible differences in taste, but most consumers when put to a taste test can rarely tell which is a well known brand and which is a supermarket own brand. In fact, when expressing their preferences in a blind tasting, consumers frequently choose the supermarket own brand product. If you think the issue of branding and brand ownership isn't really up there on the list of things to worry about, think again. Brand dominance is power, political power and financial power. Think about this for a moment. There are currently circa 460 dominant food brands in the world today, each with a substantial range of products bearing the brand identity. These brands are owned by just 10 companies. Those same companies also own thousands of less dominant brands that cater to specific geographic markets, and this is only the tip of the iceberg. If we start including non-food brands, such as personal care products and detergents, you will discover that just one of those 10 major brand owners owns 104 different brand names, and that's in addition to their 82 food brands. Another of those top 10 brand owners is a little company by the name of Coca Cola. This company virtually controls the global drinks market, but how many global or national brands do you think the Coca Cola company has a stake in? Hold on to your hats - its a staggering 590 brands spanning the whole world. Therefore, it should come as no surprise that companies in this league are able to dictate to governments on all matters that are dear to their pocketbooks. If Coca Cola decides it want's to keep pushing tons of sugar down the throats of the world's populations, then no one is going to stand in their way. Despite a world obesity epidemic, governments have only succeeded in getting these major companies to sign up to a token reduction in sugar levels in drinks and foods. These companies are so powerful that between them they can virtually dictate what each and every one of us eats, drinks, wash ourselves with, spray ourselves with, what to wash our hair with, clean our teeth with and clean our homes with.

Much of the legislation we've seen introduced by governments over packaging and product descriptions hasn't actually been put in place for the benefit of consumers. It's been put in place after full consultation with brand producers so that the packaging and descriptions used maintain the marketing objectives of those companies whilst keeping them on the right-side of any potential legal actions. One of the primary reasons for introducing health warnings on tobacco products had very little to do with government concerns over the health of the nation - after all, they didn't ban the sale of these products and continued to enjoy the huge tax revenues generated by tobacco products. Health warnings were, however, a great way to put an end to those class-action law suits against the tobacco companies who, through their advertising, had convinced consumers that smoking was "cool" and posed no danger to human health. The legislation governing what ingredients can be used in the production of various food and non-food products has also been tabled by the very industries that make these consumer goods. It allows them to fill our foods with colourants, preservatives, sugars, and all manner of other chemicals that make their products more economical to manufacture. Legally, many food stuffs can now be labeled to give us the impression that we're buying one thing, when in fact we're buying something totally different. When was the last time you went down a supermarket dairy isle to find a genuine tub or jar of of full-fat, unsweetened yogurt? The chances are you may be lucky to find just one product among the hundreds on display with names such as "greek-style" or zero fat. In some cases, some products that you may think are yogurt don't even carry the name. They are called things like "desserts". As for things such as ice cream, many of the branded products (*including some of the biggest brands in the business*) don't actually contain any significant amount of milk protein. For a product to be called ice-cream in the USA, it only has to contain 2.5% milk protein and 5% of any kind of fat, normally corn or rapeseed oil. The ingredients used don't always come from fresh produce either. Reconstituted skimmed milk and whey solids are frequently used. However, if a product is labelled as "Dairy Ice Cream", it cannot contain any vegetable fats. Instead, it must contain the obligatory 2.5% of milk protein and 5% of dairy fats. One of the principal ingredients of many ice-cream brands is palm oil. Not only is it very cheap, its also very unhealthy. This is the same substance that is extensively used in margarines, lipsticks, and detergents. It's a saturated fat that is known to be a cause of cardiovascular problems. The whey product often used to make perceived dairy products, such as cheese slices and spreadable cheeses is a by-product of the traditional cheese making process - it's the water that's left over when milk turns into cheese. It's dried into a powder and used extensively in the food industry as a very cheap protein carrier. All this non-food has largely come about through the enactment of laws that allow major food producers to create fake food. It's been allowed because it makes these food substitutes cheap to manufacture and enhances the profits made by the food industry. As for competitiveness, it often doesn't really matter what brand you purchase, the chances are very good that whatever your choice, the brands will all be owned by the same company. In other words, the brand owners compete with themselves rather than each other. So, it doesn't matter which advertising campaign convinces you to purchase a particular product, the same company often gets the sale.

One of the looming problems with having so few companies producing such large volumes of our consumer goods is that they can virtually control the supply chain for all the raw materials that go into making these products. The sheer buying power of these big companies allows them to dictate the price at which they buy the raw ingredients. They are simply too big for producers to ignore and consequently they get paid whatever the big companies are prepared to pay. Brand owning companies also set the gold-standard when it comes to the retail price of consumer goods. Those prices are not based on the actual cost of the raw materials and the cost of processing or manufacturing. Instead, they are based on consumer demand and the added brand value that these companies want. This is one of the principal reasons why identical products can be sold in different national markets at different prices. The consequence of this has a knock-on effect in the wider consumer markets. If a well known drinks brand is priced at say 60¢ a can, then that price becomes a benchmark price for the whole drinks industry. All a competing manufacturer has to do is keep the price of its product below the benchmark level established by the well known brand - maybe 39¢ a can. However, the actual cost of the product in both cases could be as low as 10¢ a can. So, the price the consumer pays has very little to do with the actual cost of the product. This process is actually eroding competition to the benefit of the major consumer brands. What is even more disturbing is that large trading blocks, such as the European Union, are helping to fuel this anti-competitive environment. Whilst goods and services can be freely moved between the member states of a trading block without the imposition of internal tariffs, the fact remains that any raw materials imported into the trading block will be subject to a common tariff which ends up as a consumer tax on goods. So, whilst there may be countries in the world that will happily provide raw materials at competitive prices, they become uncompetitive through the imposition of government tariffs. In other words, the actions of our own governments ensure that consumers end up paying more for a product than we really have to. Of course, once inside the trading bloc, the raw materials can be bought and sold by members states without the imposition of further tariffs. But, the bottom line is that the base cost of those raw materials has been artificially increased to the point where every on-cost through the production chain is increased. The UK was greatly affected by these tariffs when it first joined the EU back in 1972. At that time, the UK had trading partners the world over, specifically the ex-British colonies. Major UK sugar producers, such as Tate & Lyle could no longer import their raw cane sugar from the colonies without having to pay an EU imposed tariff and observe strict import quotas. This made the price of the company's refined sugar products uncompetitive which had the knock-on effect of significantly reducing the company's export of refined sugar products and a significant increase in the price of sugar within the UK and elsewhere in the EU. The more serious effect of this crazy EU greed, was that thousands of people lost their jobs at Tate & Lyle. The only beneficiaries of this piece of legislation were the sugar beet farmers of the EU who could now sell their inferior sugar beet tariff-free across Europe. At the same time, the EU itself found an extra source of income with which to fuel their excessive bureaucratic machine. The losers, were of course, consumers and the economies of those countries who witnessed a massive decrease in exports of their raw materials. Interestingly, the Tate & Lyle brand is now owned by a major international brand company that owns many sugar companies the world over.

So, far from a competitive environment giving us greater choice in the goods and services we buy, the reality is that competitiveness has simply concentrated power into the hands of a few well-placed companies who work hand in glove with governments to ensure consumers continue to pay ever increasing prices for the goods and services we consume. It's a nice little arrangement between large corporations and governments. Essentially, a deal is cut where the corporations will use perceived competition as a means of maintaining and steadily increase consumer prices, whilst the governments of the world keep raking in tax revenues on all that stuff we buy. In return, governments keep enacting legislation that benefits the large corporations so that they can legally maintain their dominant position in the scheme of things and fill our stomachs with stuff that human beings were simply not designed to eat. That legislation is largely dictated to governments through the powerful industry lobby groups that have far greater power over governments than the electorate at large. In another era, this would have been called a "protection racket", but in today's world, its called "competitiveness". Whilst our future revolutionaries may find this aspect of modern life a difficult nut to crack, it won't be an impossible task. Already, the ammunition is emerging that is likely to wake us all up from our consumer sleep. We're seeing increasing revelations about tainted ingredients finding their way into processed foods. We are witnessing the absolute arrogance and consumer disrespect displayed by prominent business leaders. We're starting to see the absolute food waste in modern society and we've started asking questions about the prices we're actually paying for our clothes, our furnishings, and our precious brands. The one big advantage of modern technology is that it has given us the power to be informed. We can find out where products are manufactured and at what cost. We can find out what really goes into the food we eat. We can discover very quickly just how much profit is being made by the companies that appear to be controlling our lives. Armed with this information, we're likely to see a greater exposure of the fallacy of competitiveness, but nothing will convince us more than when we discover we can no longer afford to keep supporting and paying for uncompetitive practices. That's when another phase of the real revolution will start. It will be the day when consumers reject the commercial hype and start understanding they are not getting a good deal at all. That day is coming, so be prepared.

Our Health and Happiness

We're going to start this section of the book with a quote from about BC 489. To be more precise, it's an excerpt from psalm 90 as published in the King James Version of the Bible. It goes something like this:

> *"The days of our years are*
> *threescore years and ten; and if by*
> *reason of strength they be*
> *fourscore years, yet is their*
> *strength labour and sorrow; for it*
> *is soon cut off, and we fly away"*

Now I should point out here that I'm not a particularly religious person. I respect peoples's religious believes and faiths, as long as they don't try and sell them to me. However, what I do believe is that those who contributed to the scriptures all those years ago were wise people who simply wanted to record the events of the day in order that later generations would have some idea of what went on in our ancient past, and what may be the catalyst of problems in their current lives. So, approximately 2,500 years ago, the life expectancy of the average human being was 70. (*acts of war, violence, the plague and being eaten by animals excepted*) If we made it to 80, it was, according to the scriptures, only due the grace of God who would soon come along and make sure that we didn't survive much longer than 80.

For the period 2010 - 2015, according to the world health organisation, the average health-adjusted life expectancy of human beings across the world was 71.5 years. So, despite outrageous claims by our governments that medical science has increased our life expectancy significantly, the facts would suggest otherwise. In fact. according to those health-adjusted figures, our life expectancy has increased by little more than 0.0215% over a period in excess of 2,500 years. Ok, there are regional variances and there are variances between men and women, but even if we take Japan as an example, which has one of the longest health-adjusted life expectancy rates in the world today, we see the average as 74.9 years. Countries such as the USA have quite a low a life expectancy of 69.1 years, whilst in the UK it's 71.4 years. Other Western European countries are hovering between 69 and 72 years. Of course, if we remove the health-adjusted element out of the equation, life expectancy looks much better (*one of the reasons why governments and the healthcare industry like to use non-adjusted figures*).   For example, in Japan, the figure is 83.7, for the USA it's 79.3 and for the UK it's 81.2. These undeniable statistics tell us much about the utter nonsense we are fed by our politicians. The "ageing" population is being touted as a great advertisement for the advancement of medical science. However, at the same time it's being used as an excuse for the increasing burden on society who have to meet ever increasing healthcare and pension costs for the elderly. It's also becoming a core excuse for raising retirement ages as a means of curtailing pension payouts. But, the numbers don't stack up. If we're all living longer, healthier lives, and the world population is increasing, why is there a need to raise retirement ages as a means of curtailing pension payouts? Why are healthcare costs increasing at an alarming rate? Surely, there should be sufficient social security contributions coming into the system to look after everyone and if the health of our nations is so good, why do we have higher healthcare costs. So, there must be other factors at work that we're not being told about. Therefore, we have to try and dig a little deeper in an effort to shed some light on what is really happening.

A key factor in the current state of our health is that we have wrecked the human immune system. Many of us can no longer fend off minor ailments and problems so we have to resort to the medical profession to keep us alive. The astronomical rise in obesity levels and type 2 diabetes is indicative of the fact that something has gone seriously wrong with us human beings. In the years just after World War II, it was very unusual to see an overweight person, largely due to the food rationing that came about because of the War. Yet, despite rationing, people were generally healthy. A ministry of food was even set up in the UK to ensure that we all got the essential nutrients that were needed to sustain a healthy life. The government handed out school meals to every child as part of a national policy. Those meals were nutritious and healthy meals comprising of a main course and a dessert. In some parts of the country, there was even a first course thrown in for good measure. The strange thing is that a Medical Research Council survey carried out in 1999 showed that children in the 1950's had healthier diets than children in the 1990's. The food contained more nutrients and lower levels of sugars. A free bottle of full-fat milk was also handed out to school children every day. As many of the older generation will remember, those meals always contained lots of vegetables, a good helping of meat or fish protein and deserts were often some sticky, sweet pudding with lashings of custard made from full-fat milk, and yet, obesity was a rarity. So, what went wrong?

As a child of the 50's I remember all too well how people would do their shopping. We didn't have the sprawling hypermarkets of today. Instead, every neighbourhood would have a parade of local shops, normally comprising of a butcher, fishmonger, a bakery, a greengrocer and a general provisions store. Because cars were a relative rarity back then (*and certainly women drivers were even rarer*), housewives would have to walk about one mile to their nearest shopping centre to do a daily shop (*there was no such thing as a weekly shop in those days*). The mere act of taking that daily trek and carrying the provisions back home, in itself, ensured that the housewives of the day stayed in good shape and got their required level of exercise for a healthy life. The food itself was always fresh and weighed, carved, chopped, sliced and packaged to order, so there was very little food waste through overbuying. Families would buy whatever they needed in just the right quantities to fulfil their daily needs. Towards the end of the 50's we started to see the emergence of supermarkets. These were filled with pre-packaged processed foods in tins, packets and sealed bags. Frozen foods such as vegetables also started to emerge, as too did ready meals and boil in the bag concoctions that made the housewife's life considerably easier. This evolution also meant we didn't have to visit the shops so frequently, so there was a natural decline in the amount of exercise we were getting. By the 1960's, the way people purchased food had completely changed. There was more and more industrialisation of the food industry. Intensive farming emerged in order to keep up with the demand for raw materials with which to make processed foods. Livestock was no longer allowed to roam the meadows chewing on grass. Chickens were removed from their natural surroundings and penned-up in cages housed in massive sheds. The agriculture industry were forced to increase crop yields.   All this led to the chemical companies of the day introducing all sorts of insecticides and pesticides that could be sprayed onto crops to kill off plant disease and infestations. The pharmaceutical industry also stepped into the picture to provide antibiotics that could be injected into animals who found themselves, unnaturally, hemmed together where they could develop and spread disease to each other. Livestock were being treated with hormones and steroids to increase meat or milk yields as a compensation for their lack of natural exercise. So, the situation was created where more drugs and chemicals were entering the food chain and, as a consequence, ended up inside us. The result today is that a large proportion of us are immune to the effects of possibly life-saving antibiotics.

The mid sixties also saw the emergence of another phenomena of our time - the low fat diet. Suddenly, we were all sold on the idea that saturated fats in our food would make us obese even though there was no real scientific basis for the assumption. The food industry came to the rescue with all sorts of foods that had their natural fat content stripped away. Milk was suddenly reduced from a nutritious full-fat product to a bottle of tasteless white water. There were so many nutrients stripped out of milk that the pharmaceutical companies had to come up with manufactured vitamins and minerals that could be put back into this new-found watery concoction in order to give it any form of nutritional value. Butter and solid fats that were often used for cooking and frying suddenly got replaced with vegetable oils that had been processed to look like butter (*margarine*) whilst our frying fats were replaced with vegetable cooking oils. What happened next defies belief. The world started getting fatter. Surely, the removal of fats from our diets couldn't possibly cause us all to gain weight! No, there had to be something else that happened simultaneously with this mass fat reduction in our diets. What consumers soon discovered is that removing the fat from foods, particularly meats, renders them dry and tasteless. Therefore, the food processing industry started compensating for the lack of flavour by adding sugar to the foods - most notably low cost corn sugar. This is when we started our slippery slide into mass obesity and type 2 diabetes. The food processing industry started saturating all manner of processed foods with sugars, preservatives, colourants and flavour enhancers. This had a profound impact on our diets and our health. In its attempt to strip out all the harmful bacteria to increase the shelf life of processed foods, the industry also removed all the good bacteria that we rely on to fend-off all manner of common health ailments. For those who weren't paying too much attention during biology lessons at school, the human body is, in fact, an individual eco-system. The only way to infiltrate this biological wonder we call the human body is through the skin, which is the largest organ of our bodies or, through our gut. Typically, our gut is used to absorb both good and bad bacteria which the body keeps in balance all by itself. Once manufactured and bacteria-free foods were introduced, we started to lose the ability to fight off any bad bacteria that we may inadvertently absorb into our bodies. Our natural corrective defence mechanism became underused and lazy. So much so that we've reached a point where we have to rely on the medical profession and pharmaceutical companies to compensate for our inability to fight off some of the more common ailments of our modern times.

According the the world health organisation, ailments such as obesity, diabetes, cardiovascular disease, osteoporosis, dental disease, certain cancers such as cancers of the oesophagus, stomach, colorectal, breast, endometrium and kidney can be attributable to unhealthy diet and lifestyle. With the exception of murder, misadventure or act of God, there isn't a lot left that you can die of. It seems logical to me that by getting our food intake correct and pursuing a healthier lifestyle that embodies some good old-fashioned exercise, we should be able to correct the world's health problems at a stroke. The problem is, the big food, pharmaceutical, and health care industries are making pots of money by maintaining our current levels of poor health. In the US alone, healthcare is a three trillion dollar a year industry. Add to this the fact that our foods also contain residues of poisons in the form of pesticides, herbicides and insecticides, and it will soon be realised just how much damage we are doing to ourselves and how much reliance we are placing on the pharmaceutical and healthcare industries to keep us alive. It's almost like the pharmaceutical companies are selling poison to the food and agriculture sector at the back door whilst selling the antidote to the healthcare industry at the front door. Pharmaceutical companies have also been largely responsible for breaking down the ability of our skin to protect us from harm. Almost every form of skin cleansing product, hair shampoo, sunscreen, body lotion, cosmetics and a whole host of other products, are all composed of chemicals that strip our skin of its natural protection. We see mothers chasing behind their young toddlers to wipe their hands with anti-bacterial wipes and gels after they've been caught doing what most kids do - playing in the dirt. We spray our homes with products that kill 99% of household germs. Sometimes, we need to be exposed to some of the bad things in order to build up a natural resistance to them. In recent years we've witnessed an increase in skin cancers (*melanoma*). Whilst many will blame the erosion of the ozone layer as being the chief culprit, its more likely due to our obsessive desire to strip natural oils from our skin with chemical cleaning liquids. I don't seem to recall too many skin cancers affecting farm labourers of the past who constantly worked outdoors in all weather conditions. They just developed a natural barrier to the elements through the production of melanin which gave them a protective tan that could absorb ultraviolet radiation. Nowadays, we appear to have lost the ability to combat and repair skin damage caused by UV radiation. Damage is also being caused by our sudden and rather worrying intolerances to certain foodstuffs. People actually die because they eat nuts, or they suffer from other food allergies and lactose intolerances. This is all very unnatural and should be a cause for great concern.

Our governments are fairly powerless to reign-in this madness because these industries are huge economic contributors. It's in government interests to maintain the status quo in order to keep that all-important money-go-round revolving.   It's also in government interest to offer total protection of these industries by enacting legislation that favours the companies involved. We saw this in August 2017 when it was revealed that some 700,000 eggs were released into the UK market that contained traces of Fipronil, an insecticide that can cause damage to people's kidneys, liver and thyroid glands. Whilst it was claimed at the time that the quantities found were so minuscule as to not be the cause of alarm, the fact remained that it was considered a serious enough problem for processed foods containing the tainted eggs to be removed from supermarket shelves across the EU. In fact, the European Union in its normal protective manner even criticised the 15 or so affected countries for "blaming and shaming" as such criticism wasn't "helping" the situation. Now excuse me for posing a simple question, but isn't this Fipronil poison the same stuff we squirt onto our domestic pets as a flea-control application?

Isn't this the same stuff that is impregnated into flea collars for cats and dogs? If so, why are there no controls over its use in a domestic environment where people and small children can come into contact with this stuff simply by petting their domestic animals? We should, perhaps also ask some more searching questions about this poison. One thing we do know is that it is a French pharmaceutical product, therefore it is going to have all the protection the EU can throw at it. However, it must also be a relatively inexpensive product. If it weren't inexpensive, a rogue Dutch egg producer wouldn't be able to spray thousands of battery hens with the stuff as a means of controlling flea infestations. Yet, that product when sold to consumers in the form of a flea control treatment for domestic pets cost a whopping £15 - £18 per treatment for a single animal per month - and that's at the low-end of the pricing scale. In some formulations and depending upon which country you're in, the price can be as high as £36. So, it would appear that whilst the EU has banned the substance for use in agricultural animals that are a source of food, it can be freely sold at huge profit margins to the ordinary citizens of the world to squirt onto their pets with little or no regard for the fact that the poison is likely to be ingested by pet owners and others who may come into physical contact with the animal. The reason for this absurdity? - simple! The pharmaceutical company wants its product banned in the wider livestock agriculture industry because it would be used in large quantities at a very low price (*otherwise no farmer would use it*). However, by making it available to ordinary consumers as a flea control product, they can load the price to a level that's commensurate with the consumer problem it solves. So, the EU was asked to ban the substance for wider use in the agriculture sector so that they could sell it at a premium to the great unwashed. And that's what the EU did. It's also why the EU was so angry that the farmer got caught using the stuff. His use of this product on battery hens highlighted the great rip-off price that consumers were being charged for squirting this poison on their domestic animals.

This is just one example of how governments protect the interests of the pharmaceutical industry. Another popular tactic deployed is arresting and charging individuals who promote certain natural substances that can help ward off some of those ailments we spoke about earlier. Although many of the substances promoted are fairly harmless and have some beneficial effect, people can be thrown into prison for promoting them. Governments are so afraid that someone will stumble across a natural product that can cure one or more of the big killers of our time, they will invent all sorts of legislation to prevent them spreading the news. You see, natural products cannot, by definition, be patented. Therefore, pharmaceutical companies cannot reap huge fortunes by creating commercially acceptable formulations. So, if there are no profits to be made, there will be no next big cure for anything unless it's a patented chemical formulation approved by governments. Only recently, we saw the big announcement that the US FDA had approved the first cancer treatment that modifies the patient's own immune system. It's claimed that it will leave 83% of patients free of a specific type of blood cancer. Undoubtedly, other variants of this treatment will become available to treat other types of cancers in the future. But what is this new "wonder" treatment? The pouch of liquid itself is essentially a mix of salt and sugar into which genetically modified T-cells, taken from the patient, have been added. This concoction is then fed into the bloodstream where the modified T-cells can seek out and kill cancer. The cost of this therapy is a whopping $475,000 and that doesn't include the cost of administering the stuff. So, who is likely to benefit from this therapy? For sure it won't be a treatment handed out at the taxpayer's expense in countries where publicly funded healthcare is the norm. There will probably be exceptions, such as where the patient is very young and has the potential of a very long and economically productive life ahead of them. It will also, probably, be made available to certain categories of health insurance customers, particularly those who are likely to have many years of insurance policy premium payments ahead of them. But, for the rest of us, we'll no doubt have to find the cost of the treatment ourselves, which will rather limit its use as a therapy to the very wealthy.

Whilst it isn't my intention to decry the medical industry in its entirety, I do question how we have reached a point in human evolution where we have become so reliant on drugs and treatments to deal with so many ailments. The human body, as designed by nature, was never designed to be sick and unhealthy. It was designed to be fit and healthy and have the in-built ability to take care of itself. The body does this quite naturally through the absorption of nutrients in the food we eat. The problems really started when industrialised food production became wide-spread. The nutrients found in modern foods has plummeted since the introduction of industrial food production. This means that almost everyone living in major world economies are suffering from serious nutrient deficiencies. These manifest themselves through sickness and ill-health because the body simply doesn't have the armoury to take care of itself. So, we turn to the medical profession to help us deal with the resulting symptoms. Typically, we start to get symptoms, such as a pain, a rash, feelings of lethargy or some other worrying symptom. These symptoms are the body's way of alerting us to the fact there is something wrong. So, we go to a medical practitioner who often prescribes a treatment, but the treatment is designed to tackle the symptom rather than the underlying cause of the problem.

This trend in drug reliance and nutrient deficiency is better understood when we start looking again at those life expectancy figures. In the UK, for example, it was reported in 2015 that there were a record number of people surviving to the age of 100 years. In the decade prior to 2015 the number of centenarians had risen by 65%. So, why is it, if we are living longer, that general life expectancy figures are growing at such a slow pace? It would be logical to assume that if people are living beyond 100 years, then general life expectancy should also be increasing. Well, it's all in the maths. Ordinarily, we would assume life expectancy averages to be based on adding up the ages of everyone who dies within a specific time frame (*usually one year*) and divide the resulting number by the number of people who actually died. However, that's not the way governments do it. They calculate life expectancy based upon a new born child entering the world at a particular moment in time. For this reason, life expectancy figures are constantly adjusted in line with the state of a nation's health at that chosen point in time. To see how this works, lets look at a typical person aged 60 or over. Such a person would have been born in an era prior to food industrialisation. A period prior to total dependence upon the medical profession to sort out every twitch and pain we may experience in our lives. A period prior to intensive farming and overuse of chemicals on crops. A period when farmers would use crop rotation to ensure rejuvenation of the soil so that our foods contain the maximum amount of nutrients. A period when a new born child would be fed on its mother's breast milk, immunising it from many of the more common diseases and illnesses that we could otherwise experience. So, people in their 60's are very likely to survive for many more years simply because they had a better start in life. But, what about someone in their early to mid 30's? What is their life expectancy going to be? Such people were born in an era when food industrialisation was the norm. An era when intensive farming had diminished the nutrient value of the foods we eat. An era when compulsory inoculations were forced upon every child. An era when people were encouraged to stuff themselves full of poisons, sugars, colourants, preservatives and medications to relieve the symptoms of an unhealthy body. An era when mothers fed their babies on factory-produced powdered formula which is mixed in a plastic bottle and then heated in a microwave before pouring it down the kid's throat. So, whilst a 60 year old can expect to live on until his mid to late 80's, someone in their thirties may only survive into their early 70's. This goes some way to explaining why governments need to raise retirement ages. You see, the healthy 60 year old is fit enough to carry on working and will, therefore, continue to pay taxes and make social security contributions. Whereas, someone in their 30's is likely to become so unfit prior to retirement age that they will be unable to work. In some cases, they may even die before reaching retirement.

This is a very worrying trend. The old are getting older whilst the young are dying earlier. This is creating a gap in life expectancy - a gap that appears to be widening.

Of course, many would have us believe the answer lies with medical science. Unfortunately, this isn't likely to be the case. In fact, much of the hype about the advancement of medical science is just nonsense and largely contradictory. For example, in countries where publicly funded healthcare is the norm, there is often criticism that governments are not spending enough on healthcare. The UK in particular has a healthcare crisis, yet despite massive increases in public spending in this sector, the system is under constant strain to keep up. This pressure on the healthcare system has nothing to do with lack of funding; it's all to do with one simple fact - the nation is getting sicker. Whilst governments would never admit this, preferring instead to blame the elderly for using up valuable resources because they are all living longer, they continue to feed us the line that we are all healthy and fit and that our well being is all down to advancements in medical science. The truth is that the only people who benefit from increased government spending on healthcare are the pharmaceutical companies and those who manufacture medical equipment. Essentially, medical science has been part of the problem. The constant bombardment of drugs into our bodies to relieve the symptoms of our unhealthy lifestyles has simply served to exasperate the problem. Instead of dealing with the underlying medical issues that are making us sick, medical science has simply masked the symptoms. As such, we've become totally dependent upon pills and potions. In today's world, many of us have little choice in opting out from this cycle of "poison and antidote". When a newborn child arrives in the world, it is usually given a very large natural immunisation shot against all manner of nasties through the process of natural childbirth. Sadly, in today's world, babies are born with close on 300 chemicals in their bodies which they inherit from their mothers. All those chemicals are specifically designed to render the body's natural defence mechanisms fairly useless. The problem is then compounded by the fact that many women now choose C-section births that deprive the new born of even that initial immunisation. So, it's straight out of the womb into the hands of the medical profession who often immediately hook the child up to drips or subject it to jabs to get even more chemicals into its system. Right from the very first moment of human life, babies are becoming ever more dependent upon medical science to ensure they reach their threescore years and ten. This is taking its toll at a much higher level than we may imagine. In nature, any species, whether it be plant life or animal, that cannot survive in its natural environment is usually subjected to nature's own natural selection process. Its ability to reproduce becomes affected and, in some cases, results in whole species being wiped out. It is, therefore, probably no coincidence that one in four couples in the world today are unable to conceive without some form of medical intervention. That's a staggering figure and should be sounding the alarm bells. Although we are probably a long way off total extinction, we are well on our way to the natural selection process. This will mean that the ability of future generations to conceive and have children will be decided by the parent's ability to pay for specialist medical help. At worst, it may even be decided by governments through legislative changes that favour giving specialist help only to those who are likely to produce a genetically perfect offspring.

To make matters worse, many of us have also lost the art of cooking. We literally destroy our foods, even when we are preparing fresh produce. We boil the life out of our vegetables, removing many of the remaining nutrients they contain in the process. Leaf vegetables only really need a quick blanch in boiling water. Root vegetables are a little trickier to soften up, but even they can be gently steamed until they become tender. The advent of the non-stick pan has also given us other dangers to worry about. You would be surprised how many people add vegetable oil to a non-stick pan and then bring it up to temperatures in excess of 200° celsius before adding food to the pan. Firstly, non-stick coatings can break down at these high temperatures, releasing all sorts of nasties into our food. Secondly, vegetable oils should never be brought up to these high temperatures for frying. Heating most vegetable oils such as sunflower, soy, and corn above 180° celsius leads to the release of high concentrations of aldehydes (*20 times higher than WHO recommendations*) which have been linked to cancer, heart disease and dementia. The oils recommended for low temperature frying are light olive oils (*non-extra virgin*) and rapeseed oil. Whilst olive oil has the potential of releasing toxins, it's usually at a much lower level than the other vegetable oils. Rapeseed oil, and its genetically modified equivalent, Canola, can be used for frying quite safely. Another good vegetable oil that can be used is coconut oil. However, since it became well known that this was a safe cooking oil, the price has soared through the roof, making it too expensive for most people. So, what should be used for frying? Many experts are saying that good old animal fats are the best as they are the least likely to release toxins. They can withstand some very fierce temperatures and yet remain safe to cook in. Lards, butter (*particularly Ghee*) and goose fat are considered by many experts to be the safest frying medium. As for sunflower, soy and corn oil, it's been recommended to not use them at all - not even for salad dressings. If you need to use cold oils go for extra virgin olive oil on your salads and pasta.

We've also been sold on the idea that we must overcook our meats in order to destroy harmful bacteria. If truth be told, we're more likely to be adversely affected by the stuff injected into meats than we are to be affected by harmful bacteria. Most bacteria in meats are only on the surface. Therefore, a good wash is normally sufficient to make it safe. Searing meat at high temperatures also has the same effect. As for the cooking itself, most meats do not need to be cooked beyond an internal temperature of 62° celsius to make them totally safe without destroying the protein. You only have to watch a good professional chef at work to understand how correct cooking in the correct mediums create a better tasting, more nutritional dish. There are new schools of thought emerging that suggest that all our health problems are caused by us eating meat and fish proteins. Whilst I am no scientist or medical researcher, I do question the validity of this type of argument. I don't have a problem with people choosing to not eat meat and fish on ethical grounds. However, I really do have a problem with those who claim we shouldn't eat these proteins on health grounds. My reasoning is based on evidential facts. Human beings have been eating fish and meat proteins for thousands of years and yet it is only over the past 60 years or so that we seem to have developed health problems that are now being attributable to the consumption of meat and fish. In the animal kingdom, where the killing and consumption of live prey is the norm, we rarely see animals such as lions and tigers suffering from cardiovascular disease or cancers. We don't see their immune systems so weakened that they have to rely on constant visits to doctors to make them better. It doesn't make sense to simply blame a specific form of protein that has been consumed by human beings for so long without ill effect. Of course, there is probably a great deal of merit in the argument that processed meat and fish proteins can cause us harm. The unnatural ingredients used in the production of processed meats, along with all the other chemical compounds and drugs that find their way into the base ingredient may well be a cause for significant concern. But the notion that meat and fish in itself is something that should be avoided simply doesn't ring true with me. When I look at those fortunate few in the world that can afford to eat meat, fish and dairy products that are totally devoid of human interference, I see people who live very long and, largely, healthy lives. The UK's Royal family have their own farms to produce the food they eat and have a diet rich in protein. They eat wild venison, wild salmon, naturally grazed lamb and beef, eggs, milk and all manner of vegetables that have all been totally untouched by the pharmaceutical or chemical industries. They are all healthy and living long lives, so what is so different about their diet to the diets the rest of us have to endure? You've guessed it - they don't eat foods that have been processed outside of the family kitchens or outside approved processing businesses, such as traditional butchers and cheesemakers. They know every ingredient that goes into their food.

It's all frightening stuff and our next revolutionaries are going to have to deal with these important issues. I guess they could start by demanding the food we eat hasn't been genetically modified, or sprayed with poison. They could boycott all foods that have been packed with additives and chemicals. They could also boycott all intensely farmed products, particularly meat products where animals have been raised in cramped conditions and who need antibiotics and other drugs to ensure they survive the ordeal. They will have to launch massive education initiatives to enlighten the world what has happened to them and what they can do to correct the imbalances created by our massive food, agriculture and medical industries. It won't be an easy job, but one that will form a central part of any forthcoming revolution.

The Business of Religion

I guess a book about how our historic past has been a major influence over our current human conditioning wouldn't be complete without a mention of the taboo subject of religion. As I said in a previous chapter, I'm not a particularly religious person, but I do understand the importance that religion has in the lives of many people. In times of distress and sorrow, religion helps many overcome the negative impact of sadness and grief. People obtain great comfort and a sense of reasoning through a religious belief system - no matter what religion it may be. People also need a sense of belonging and a church congregation can provide that all important sense of being part of a community. Whilst scientists have offered up irrefutable evidence on the origins of man and the evolution of our planet, people still need to believe in a higher authority that, it is claimed, made it all possible. For these reasons, I would never decry anyone's religious beliefs, even if I don't share them. The basic problems with religious belief systems is that they have been crafted by mere men who sought to exercise power over the masses. Most religions are based on, fundamentally, the same scriptures that were written thousands of years ago. The scholars of the day wrote, what they considered to be, a historic record of facts as they saw them. Because there was a lack of higher understanding of what was happening around them, some put their own interpretation on the events recorded. The term "miracle" was used to describe events that were difficult to give any logical reasoning to. Apparitions, although maybe occurring quite naturally, couldn't be explained with any degree of reasoning. Had the events of the day happened a few thousand years later, scholars may have been able to explain things in a completely different manner and with a higher degree of understanding. As it was, we got our scriptures that were meticulously handed along, generation after generation, century after century until they finally found themselves in the hands of organised churches.

Churches, of all faiths, really only came about as a means of exercising power. They represented the original politicians or, worked closely with ruling dynasties to ensure their prominent place in society, controlling populations the world over. Some churches were not even particularly nice. The famous Catholic inquisitions of Rome, Spain and Portugal were particularly nasty and vicious affairs that sought to eradicate all manner of other religious beliefs as well as paganism and witchcraft. Yet, strangely enough, the Catholic church, along with other Christian churches adopted many of the Pagan rituals that were so popular in Europe. The winter solace became Christmas, The Ostara celebrations, which focused on the theme of renewal and rebirth, became Easter. Each church put their own spin on these pagan celebrations and directly related them to events recorded in their scriptures. So, Churches, rather than the underlying religions, became very powerful. They constructed huge edifices and filled them with all manner of treasures. Their leaders and clergy cloaked themselves in intimidating gowns and headgear and wore large opulent jewels and gold chains. They built palaces full of works of art, statues, gold and silver artefacts, all designed to intimidate and give the impression of great power. In many countries, Churches were given national status as "official" churches to the state. Churches were given, or in some cases, helped themselves to, huge estates and properties. The churches became seriously wealthy and didn't really contribute much to the spiritual well being of their followers. The expression "the fear of God" springs to mind. Most people followed their religion out of fear of persecution or the fear that they may lose their place in the afterlife and become subjected to an eternity in the fire and brimstone world of the Devil.

It isn't without reason that churches were able to coexist alongside ruthless rulers. Those rulers were just as intimidated by the apparent powers of the churches and their religious leaders as the guy in the street. So much so that they actually thought that jumping into bed with a Church would somehow exonerate them from the torturous afterlife that could befall them for all the sins they committed during their life. They gave churches great power to collect money, to exempt them from taxes, to hold court over the lives of ordinary people, and in many cases, the power to torture and execute those who defied the church. Although the days of religious persecution are largely over, churches still enjoy many of the monetary benefits bestowed upon them by rulers of the past. They still seek to dictate to us what we should and shouldn't do. Long gone are the days when we were simply quoted the ten commandments as a guide to how we should live our lives. In today's world, churches seek to dictate all manner of things, such as the use of contraception, the right to have an abortion, whether we are considered worthy of a religious wedding ceremony, a Christening or a church funeral service. And whilst they still go about their business, we see church leaders covering up or being involved in the sexual and physical abuse of children - even within the past 50 years. We see them still amassing huge tax-exempt wealth which never seems to be put to good humanitarian use. We see churches locking up their edifices just in case a homeless person wanders in and decides to bed down for the night. We see them voicing their opinion over government cuts, inequalities and the scourge of big business. They may be right to be critical, but given their huge wealth, maybe they should use some of that money to help out some of the world's less fortunate instead of simply preaching from the pulpit about what everyone else is doing wrong. Churches, not religions, are big business. They still seek to dictate and they still amass wealth. They are supported wholeheartedly by governments and monarchs the world over.

Whilst I wouldn't advocate the abolition of Churches, I would advocate making them more accountable. Start by making them pay taxes on their huge profits. Insist that a percentage of their income be used for good humanitarian purposes in exchange for tax breaks. Force them to submit annual returns for their congregations to scrutinise - after all, it's their money, just like shareholders in a big company.   Churches should also be prevented from "forgiving" in the name of their respective religions those who commit atrocities and gross acts of violence. We saw in the past where ruthless mafia families were protected by the Church and absolved of their crimes, even though they would often walk away from the confessional box and go commit even more crimes. Those who have been radicalised into committing horrendous acts of terror in the name of religion should be denounced by the churches in whose name they commit their terrible acts. Whilst churches are free to "forgive and absolve" we're unlikely to see the decline of hate crimes committed in the name of religion.

It is often said that just about every war had religion at its root cause, the truth is it has been the man-made churches and their leaders who have been instrumental in pursuing an often violent agenda. Nowhere do we see religious texts from any faith in which violence, murder or acts of terror form any part of their respective teachings. Our next revolutionaries will have to tackle the issue of Churches and their true role in society. By all means, lets give them the job of looking after our spiritual needs. Let's allow them to have their pomp and ceremonies and let's allow them to be critical of our political masters. But, what we also need to do is strip them of their huge financial power. We must stop them amassing warehouses full of valuable artefacts that have been paid for by their congregations. We should stop them from constructing ever larger edifices that only serve to intimidate people, or to focus religious hatred upon themselves. If you go to Russia, Turkey, Greece or the UK, you will find churches costing hundreds of millions being built today. Each one is a symbol of power that their respective churches simply cannot resist exhibiting. They feel that by building a bigger, more opulent church within eyeshot of another church selling a different religion, they will be perceived as more dominant and more powerful. It has nothing to do with creating churches large enough to accommodate an expanding population of church-goers. Many churches find it difficult to get the first three rows of even the smallest parish church filled with people on one day of each week. It's all about the display of wealth and power. This has to come to an end in order for ordinary people to start coming together as equals to make the world a better place. Get the churches out of the business of high finance and property development. Get them out of the "business" of religion and into a world where they can do the most good - giving us support and comfort in our hours of need, and giving us a less intimidating place of worship where congregations can meet with like minded people and celebrate their religions. If they do this, then they may manage to convert people like me to their faith. But whilst they have the appearance of a greedy group of privileged business people who care little about anyone but themselves, they won't get me as convert any time soon.

Where to Next

It would be inconceivable to think that the whole world will rise to the challenge of launching a coordinated global revolution any time soon. Therefore, the best we can hope for is a more fragmented approach to getting our discontent recognised by our elected "dictators". We're already seeing signs of this, particularly in Europe. The revolution appears to have already started. The election of Trump to the White House, the reelection of Merkel in the 2017 elections in Germany with the far right taking a larger share of the vote, the reelection of UK premier Theresa May in 2017 with a significantly reduced majority and the mutterings of discontent in a number of European countries are all showing signs of changes to come. Traditionally, in most western democracies, party politics has always taken centre stage. Parties are either right-leaning or left-leaning. What elections in 2017 started to illustrate is that the ordinary citizen is becoming increasingly angry at this arrangement. Election results are showing political parties gaining power with ever narrowing majorities. It's almost as if ordinary people are forcing political parties into the centre ground. This is a more noticeable phenomenon in countries where there has always been a two party system of politics, but it's also becoming apparent in countries where coalition governments are the norm, such as Germany. In the

2017 elections, German citizens, for the first time ever, decided to give a degree of power to the far right AfD party, a political movement that is seen as being racist and nationalistic. Whilst German voters, clearly, didn't want this grouping to have a majority in the Bundestag, they did appear to want to level the playing field by giving none of their political parties a clear majority. The best way to achieve this was to bring in the AfD with their radical views and policies. As you would expect, no other political grouping will work with the AfD in order to form a majority government, so they will still be marginalised and left in the wings as a minor political force. However, the political message is still there, loud and clear. People want change. They want their voices heard and they expect today's politicians to listen and act accordingly.

Tragically, we live in a world today that is dominated by political agendas. We no longer elect politicians based upon what they can do for us as individuals. We elect them based on a political manifesto that's conjured up by a bunch of party mandarins who head up the political party that the representative is a member of. We may not agree with everything in that manifesto, but we tend to "balance the books" and go for the party that is more leaning towards our individual ideology. The problem is that manifesto pledges often remain undeliverable, so we see politicians enacting all those bits of manifestos that we don't agree with, whilst ignoring all the policies that we voted for. Therefore, we have to start making our elected representatives more accountable to us as individuals. We could start by actually meeting with the candidates prior to an election. We should be brave enough to tell them what we think of their manifesto and to start asking them if they have any intention of listening to the ordinary citizens they claim to represent. If they tell us that we will simply be voting for the pledges made in their manifesto, we should tell them to take a hike - we are not voting for a series of pledges that have little or no impact on our personal lives. We have to be prepared to remind them that we want to vote for someone who will act as our voice at national level. The last thing we want is to vote for someone who is simply on a career path within his or her political party. If we can tear down the political party system and start voting for representatives who will duly represent the constituents that put them in a position of power, we will be well on our way to a true democracy again.

Leaving politics to one side, we can also start instigating our own revolution by simply refusing to be followers. Instead of responding to media and corporate hype, we should start making decisions based on what we think is right for us and our families.   We should slow down on our embracement of new technologies that will ultimately replace human beings in the work place. We should stop using social media to broadcast our personal lives to the whole world. Nobody in their right mind would leave the door to their home wide open 24/7 for fear that those that would do us harm or steal from us will simply walk in and do their damage. And yet, that's precisely what many people do with their online life. They leave themselves exposed to anyone who wants to walk into their personal space and do harm. Whether it's to flood your email inbox with countless offers of junk products, or if it's people who will simply abuse you or make derogatory comments about you, it's still an invasion into your personal territory to either harm you or to get money out of you. One thing that we should all do is to crank up the privacy settings on our technology devices, particularly those that are driven by Microsoft Windows or Android. These platforms are little more than gateways into your personal life. They allow all sorts of strangers to infiltrate your personal space for commercial exploitation. They even use the weaknesses of these operating systems to infect your computers, tablets and smartphones with viruses and malware that can completely cripple your devices.

We should also be a little more aware of the marketing hype deployed by big-brand companies and the retailers that sell their products. In many respects, we need to wear blinkers when we shop in big supermarkets, just like race horses do at the racetrack. If we can put all the special offers and promotions out of our line of sight and just buy the things we went to the store to buy, we would all be wealthier in an instant. And, talking of supermarkets, start eating healthier. Forget all that pre-packed and factory made food you see littering the supermarket shelves. Our children are not trash cans, so stop shoving garbage into them. Not only will you give them the opportunity of a healthy and long life, you'll also save a fortune on medical bills (*or the taxpayer's social welfare costs if you live in a country where healthcare is provided by the state*). You may have to spend an extra 15 minutes in the kitchen preparing good nutritional food, but surely your family is worth that little bit of effort. When it comes to the education of our children, we should all stop leaving our kids education to chance. We should start taking a more proactive role by signing up for and attending PTA meetings. If your child's school doesn't have a PTA - start one and get your voice heard where it matters.   When we look at the best performing education systems at elementary level in the world today, one country stands out - Finland. This country has consistently ranked as one of the best education systems in the world and yet, the students only do a 20 hour week, rarely get homework and have a much wider curriculum than many other countries in Europe and the USA. They've also done away with standard testing of children which only serves to pigeonhole students into specific groups that get a different education to others. Of course, these tests are also a sort of benchmarking for educational establishments. This means that parents in most countries have to search out the best schools if they want their children to have the best education. This doesn't happen in Finland. All schools are equal and there is no segregation of students into "ability" groups. In the UK, they have a somewhat strange education system. It's generally an ability-based system that sets out to segregate students into those that perform well, and those that don't perform quite as well. Schools also get a ranking based on how well they educate the young. This is absolutely crazy and is something that can only be stopped by parents. Unfortunately, the UK education authorities, in an attempt to stop parents from seeking out better schools have now downgraded exams so as to give a higher chance of passing them. This in turn leads to a better score for the schools so that parents will feel it's a better school than it really is. This is all part of the "competitiveness" that the UK government so embraces in everything from education, healthcare right through to the provision of public transport and utilities. It's a system that is doomed to failure, but if we continue to embrace this nonsense, little, if anything, will change.

Finally, we have to do something about the obscenities of the financial markets. If we all stopped participating in crazy investment schemes, stocks and shares, government bonds and all the other financial instruments that are supposed to increase our wealth, we would see a complete breakdown of the lunacy in the "money-for-nothing" regime.   Think about it, buying stocks and shares doesn't actually create anything - it's just a mechanism that moves money from the pockets of one sector of society to another. Buying stocks in Microsoft or any other major corporation, isn't actually creating new jobs, more products or serving to make economies any wealthier. It's simply a secondary market where the losers hand over their cash to the winners. The companies whose stocks and shares are being traded receive no intrinsic added value other than the fact that their major shareholders see the value of their investment rising or falling in line with the lunatic valuations being placed on these instruments.   We know this for a fact as pension schemes who invest predominantly in the secondary markets are consistently failing to meet the financial needs of their contributors. This situation is made worse by the fact that the whole financial industry is made up of people who all have their hands held out for a fee or commission from each and every transaction carried out. Stockbrokers get commissions (*win or lose*), fund managers get paid fees and commissions, Investment banks get paid fees and commissions, Lawyers get huge fees for preparing all those convincing documents and contracts that part us from our hard-earned money and accountants get massive fees for telling us that all is right with our investments even when everything is going pear-shaped. When I look at people like Bernard Madoff, who ran a multi-billion dollar Ponzi scheme for the best part of 17 years, I see a very sad story. Ok, the guy was a crook and he will spend the rest of his life behind bars, but he did bring the message home to those who were gullible enough to seek the easy-money route in life. Some of the biggest names in the financial world were drawn into his scheme. Sadly, many smaller investors who trusted their so-called professional advisors also lost their savings overnight. But, the real wake up call was for the big institutional investors and high-net-worth individuals who entrusted their money to this con-man. Do we feel sorry for them? Not really. These are the people who fleece ordinary people all the time, so I feel no sympathy whatsoever for them. In many respects, we should be thanking people like Bernard Madoff for highlighting the lunacy of the system. We should thank him for showing us that the so-called smart professionals of the financial markets cannot be trusted. They, like most human beings, simply follow the smell of easy-money and, yet, our governments and regulatory institutions try to convince us that we should always trust an authorised financial advisor. They hand out licences to people who are no more clever than the ordinary guy in the street. It seems our governments want to force us into the hands of incompetent people who can flaunt the law with impunity and simply steal our money. Wake up world and smell the coffee!

In concluding this foray into the world we live in today we should understand something very important. We do not need any more bloody revolts in order to get our voices heard. All we need to do is take action with the tools we've been given. We have to sweep aside all that propaganda that has evolved from our recent history and start viewing the world for what it is. Forget the torrents of misinformation (*or fake news*) that we are fed every day. Put it all to the back of your minds and start seeing the world from your perspective. Start implementing changes to your individual lives and start asking awkward questions of our politicians. Resist the temptation to judge other people and situations by the messages sent out by today's media. Start thinking on your feet and acting accordingly. By doing this, you will be part of a new revolution that is set to change our lives and the course of history yet again. Do nothing and you can say goodbye to the future of your children and their children. Nothing is insurmountable, so start small with your own private revolution and others will start getting the message.